# Angel with Drumsticks

*The rock that shook the foundations of the Vatican*

*By Pamela King*

Published by Ferrari 2014

ISBN: 978-09875412-3-9

www.angelandthebrains.com

# Contents

# Contents

# Preface

When I told Angelo Ferrari I wanted to write the story of the band his response was:

> *"Well.... you want to know my story and the truth about the Mass Beat? The story of how the Vatican ruined the career of young musicians? I will tell you the true story and not the fantasies of the many media reports."*

This is the story as it was told to me by Angelo Ferrari, drummer, singer and founder of the Italian rock group Angel and the Brains. In researching support information for this book, I have discovered considerable information that is incorrect, not the least of which has emanated from the Catholic Church.

The story tells of young musicians, good Catholic boys, who responded to an invitation from a church representative to fulfil the new desires of the Vatican II to be more appealing to young people, only to be excommunicated and have their promising careers ruined before they reached manhood.

There are many articles written about the church backpedalling on the aim of Vatican II, but there are no articles that we have been able to find outlining the Vatican's immediate response to the Mass, its actions and the repercussions. This story has only been made possible through the recollections of people who experienced the injustices.

Some of the names in this story have been changed to protect the privacy and security of innocent people.

A lot of the research material for this book was taken from Italian text. Every attempt has been made to accurately retain the message of the text during translation.

I would like to express my sincere appreciation to my editor, Jennifer Edmonds, for her valuable suggestions and friendship.

*Pamela King*

# 1. Not just any rock concert

The young men fidgeted behind stage, waiting for the seats to fill and their signal to begin. This was to be the biggest concert yet in their fledgling music careers, and each one was filled with that curious mixture of excitement flavoured with nervousness that comes from such an event. They had practised until they were flawless—their fingers knew every chord change, their voices every harmony, they had been living and sleeping and dreaming this moment for weeks and they were as ready as they could ever be—yet still the hearts fluttered lightly and breath was occasionally short; they knew that this was an important milestone.

Three bands, all comprising young men, would share the stage, and each take their turn at the songs they had been allotted until the last number, which they would perform together. They had never worked together before—this was the first time they had ever met—and they wondered how their very different and distinctive styles would play out together on stage.

As they waited, they could hear the concert hall filling.

Just over two hours earlier, when their car had pulled up outside the forbidding building designed by 17th Century architect Borromini, the young band members stared at the intimidating building and took a collective deep breath. Angelo dropped his cheek into the palm of his hand. "Well, we are here, I hope everything goes alright".

It had been a typical Roman spring day. *Aprile dolce dormire* is an Italian expression meaning 'April sweet sleep'. In Rome it is a beautiful mid-spring month, the days are usually fresh, mostly sunny or partly cloudy. It is known as a month for quiet relaxation and great for day trips or short holidays.

Now, as the bands launched into their music— delighting their audience with their new beat, their new style, their new *way*—the gentle spring air was shattered, the music was so loud it could be heard kilometres away. Even the thunderous Italian traffic with its constant discordant harmony of horns could not be heard in the forecourt of the Oratorium let alone inside the hall itself.

The 2,000-seat auditorium had no pre-booked seating and it was a matter of first in, first served. The organisers had been hopeful of a healthy turnout, but even their most optimistic assessments were shattered when over 10,000 turned up, and around 8,000 were turned away from the doors of the already full hall. Speakers were hastily erected outside for the benefit of these eager young fans, who jostled and crowded on the outside, desperate to hear the sounds of their favourite band.

The national Italian television station, RAI, set up their television cameras to record the occasion and police lines were unable to contain the horde of youngsters who, motivated by this new and vital mystical feeling, had swamped the seats, tables and cornices to insure those few centimetres of space needed to wiggle their limbs.

The boom of the drums and bass sounded like a thunder storm about to hit—and it was.

The 8,000 fans, mostly young people, who couldn't get into the venue, were intoxicated by the sounds coming from the huge speakers that had been hastily set up so everyone could still hear the music being performed inside.

Inside, the applause was nearly as loud as the music and young girls were screaming with tears running down their faces as they jostled to get a closer glimpse of their new music heroes and, if at all possible, touch them.

As the words and the music drew the crowd in, eager for more, the musicians were both astounded and elated by the adulation and excitement of the crowd.

The young musicians of Angel and the Brains had practiced industriously, perfecting their talent and style. They had already enjoyed some success with their new Italian beat but this was a phenomenal response to their new style. "At last our music is being received well," the young Angelo Ferrari thought to himself as they handed over to the next band on the stage, and wished with all his heart that his band were performing more than their allotted four songs.

At 6pm the temperature was still a warm 20 degrees. Inside the Oratorium, the crowd of 2,000 people, RAI's lighting and the stage lighting added to the intensity of the heat. Inside it was hot, airless and smoke filled, but the audience in their frenzy didn't seem to notice.

Members of Angel and the Brains had hoped that this concert would go well, and launch their music careers, and it seemed that their hopes and dreams were to be realised this night. They could have no way of knowing that this concert that would see them rocket to the dizzy heights of fame, would also be the cause of their ultimate failure.

What the bands and the fans didn't know back then in 1966 was that a religious furore would follow this performance, for this was no ordinary rock concert; it was the world's first rock Mass and the venue for this extraordinary concert was not an ordinary concert hall or outdoor stadium but in fact a Catholic Church—the St. Filippo Neri Oratorium, Sala Borromini in Piazza della Chiesa Nuova 18, Rome.

It would be the first—and last—time that rock music would be heard from within the hallowed walls of a Catholic Church in Rome.

## 2. How did I get here

On stage at the Mass, while waiting to perform his next song, Angelo pondered his journey to this point. It had been such a brief time since he had decided in 1962 at the age of 14 he wanted to play music and make it his career.

It had begun some years earlier when his mother had interrupted his television watching to announce, "I have arranged for a piano teacher to come once a week so you can learn to play."

The ten year old had groaned, "Why?"

"Because everyone needs to learn some cultural skill", she replied. "Don't groan like that, your sister will also be learning ballet".

That made Angelo grin as he chuckled to himself, "That will be a big joke!"

Although he complained at first about the lessons, Angelo quickly took to music and when he got bored with repetitive practising of piano scales, he would experiment with different chords and sing along to his own music, writing down songs as he created them.

Angelo's mother had been a soprano and her father a tenor. She recognised the boy's talent and passion and once again decided it was time for lessons. She said to him, "Well, if you like to sing you better learn how."

His father spoke to a well-known singing teacher, hoping he would train his son in voice. "I don't just take anyone," the teacher warned. "You had better bring him along so I can hear him,"

Angelo was very nervous but the teacher quickly put him at ease asking gently, "What would you like to sing?"

"*Un Angelo non sei*," replied Angelo, with nerves fluttering in his stomach. "Do you know it? It is a Little Tony song."
"Yes, I know it," smiled the maestro.

Angelo sang while the teacher accompanied him on the piano. When he finished, the teacher turned enthusiastically to Angelo's father and announced, "I'll take him, he has a voice!"

In addition to his piano lessons Angelo now started singing lessons once a week.

He was often left alone at home but was never lonely when he had music to play. He enjoyed it and it was an escape for him trying new passes and chords. He often wrote songs down just for his own enjoyment.

As he watched television or listened to the radio he thought to himself, "I can do better than that!" The quiet music rebel inside had started to emerge, showing signs of what was to come.

After taking formal singing lessons for a year and a half and learning keyboard he also tried the bass guitar but decided it was not for him.

*Angelo at 15 years old*

Between the ages of 14 and 16 he performed as a solo singer in theatres and as a support artist to bigger name performers in concerts in small towns.

Angelo remembered the first time he was booked to sing by himself.

"I was so nervous. I remember so clearly the variety theatre where I performed for a week alongside other performers including comedians, a juggler, magician and dancers.

"It was at the Teatro Ambra Jovinelli. I was fascinated by the design of the building. It was the only one in Rome built in the Art Nouveau style and intended as a comedy theatre."

*Teatro Ambra Jovinelli*

In 1962 some cinemas had a live show before the movie started so at that time it was actually a theatre and cinema in one.

"I performed three songs every evening and twice on Sunday. All I can remember about the dancers is that their legs were as long as I was tall!"

He recalled the kindly comedian who was in charge and remembered him telling the stage manager, "Don't put the young singer on after me. The last thing this kid needs is people laughing when he comes on stage."

Angelo says, "I ended up performing between the juggler and the magician.

"I was paid good money that week. It was equivalent to a month's pay for an average worker at the time.

"The other performers were part of a variety troupe that travelled around Italy performing at various venues. At the end of the week they invited me to join them but I still had school and a lot more to learn about music."

About a month later his maestro, who had got him the job in the theatre, suggested he enter a festival song competition in the small southern Roman town of Rocca di Papa.

"I competed against 25 other singers who performed a variety of songs and I won the festival.

"I then went to stay for a while with some priests in Rieti, a city north of Rome. The priest who baptised me knew I was singing and had invited me to visit.

"We had a party there and every night enjoyed a beautiful dinner. One special moment was when I met the mayor of the town who asked me to perform at a big festival they were holding.

"In autumn, my maestro got me another contract. This time I was performing all night, every night for a month in a night club. I was the youngest performer there but everyone was very nice to me. I went on stage five or six times every night singing for about half an hour each time I was on stage."

He chuckled, "Oh, I remember how hard it was to drag myself out of bed to go to school each day because I was performing from nine p.m. until three in the morning!

"At that time there was very little rock and roll in Italy so I was still performing the old traditional Italian songs."

Maybe it was the combination of the quality of his voice for his age that made him appeal to the traditional audiences, but he was not happy and he considered the music boring and of little challenge.

The music he enjoyed listening to the most was by some of the new Italian artists of the time who he considered young, innovative and interesting. These artists included Adriano Celentano, Little Tony and Bobby Solo.

He smiled to himself as he recalled watching the first of the rock-and-roll performers in Italy in the 50s, Adriano Celentano, perform on stage. Celentano jumped up and down all the time and people started calling him 'The Spring' and he was great fun to watch. However, Angelo felt that Little Tony and Bobby Solo's songs were more his style and focused on their music. He said, "Little Tony was more gentle in his rock technique than 'The Spring'. Bobby Solo styled himself like Elvis Presley with a similar hairstyle and moves, but I always thought his voice was much better than Elvis's and in my opinion his songs were a lot nicer, too."

Angelo did concentrate more on songs from Little Tony and Bobby Solo and their style did seem to suit him. He even did cover versions of the two artists in his performances.

When not at school, singing lessons or performing, Angelo continued to sit at his piano and write his own songs. He tried recording one of his songs but as he was still only 15 he did not have any success. But he didn't let it didn't stop him continuing to compose.

After discovering the new style of music being sung in Italy, he finally had songs he liked and could be included in his repertoire but he still wasn't completely happy. No matter who was singing, young or old, they were being backed by musicians from the 1940s. "That's when I decided I needed my own group.

I needed to be able to give them the music and make sure it was the right music for the day."

Talking to one of his friends about the music of the time Angelo said, "If anyone really listens to music from the 1940s and 1950s—not just Italian music, but from all over the world—they would realise that there were a lot of instruments being used. This was fine in the 40s and a good part of the 50s because it meant there was a full orchestra backing the singer and 25 to 30 musicians playing a wide range of instruments.

"But look what has happened. The bands got smaller and smaller in the latter part of the 1950s until there were only four or five people playing instruments. Something else is needed to fill the sound because a guitar, keyboard or organ by itself cannot fill up the whole music or the whole song."

As a solo artist, Angelo had to rely on backing musicians who were, without exception, used to playing 1940s-style music and unable to produce the energy in their music that he craved.

After coming off stage one day, having been backed by one of these bands, he told his father, "There are gaps everywhere in the music and there is no beat! I can't perform my songs the way I think they should be. I need a band with beat and enthusiasm behind me. I need somebody I can practice with and in the end I can trust when we are performing."

"That's fine, but how do we start to do that?" his father asked.

"First find somewhere to practice, then spread the word that we are looking for musicians to join a band," Angelo replied.

"I think I know someone that can help with a room to practice," his father mused, giving it some thought.

"That's great!" said Angelo. "I'll tell some friends that we are looking for good musicians, but I don't want anyone over 20 years old".

"It will be not easy to get good musicians so young," cautioned his father.

"Let me worry about that. I'm sure I can get them and they will play my way," laughed Angelo.

## 3. Band formation

Angelo had decided two years earlier that music would be his career and as he was just finishing school in 1964 he decided the time was right to form his band. He was living at home and had the support and encouragement of his parents.

He went to his friends and told them about his idea. "I want to get a band together. Do you know anyone who might be interested?"

"I know someone who is really good on the guitar but doesn't like to practice on his own so he might be interested," said Umberto thoughtfully.

"Wow that's exciting. I too know someone who plays guitar and would be really good in a band," said Giorgio

The first musician they found was Ruggero Coletta, a guitar player the same age as Angelo. He was a very good guitarist and had his own ideas about music as well as being good at arrangements. He was the ideal musician for the new band.

Angelo asked him, "Are you ready to create a new style of music?"

"Yes, I have been looking for an opportunity like this. I've had enough of listening to the same style of music all the time and I've come to dislike conservatory-trained musicians", he replied eagerly.

They decided to get together once a day to try to find more musicians for the band.

The second band member was Maurizio Vitti. He wasn't as skilled with the guitar as Ruggero but he already had a beat sound in his playing style.

"What do you think is your best attribute as a musician?" Angelo asked him.

"I am good at following the band leader, providing the leader will follow my beat." He smiled.

Angelo looked at him. He was enthusiastic and a good musician but even to Angelo he looked very young. "Just how old are you?" Angelo asked him.

"I'm fourteen, almost fifteen," bragged the young guitarist.

"Are you still at school?" Ruggero asked him.

"I just finished junior high," Maurizio told him. He turned to Angelo. "Look, if you are worried about my commitment, just give me a try. I will prove to you I am committed."

Still a bit doubtful, Angelo smiled at him. "When we

find some more members we'll give you a try and see what happens."

"I know a keyboard player that may be interested," Maurizio said, keen to be part of the group and get started.

"Good," said Ruggero, "tell him to come along too."

Angelo and the other kids met and discussed music at length. They all felt the music of the day was dreary the way it was being performed most of the time and agreed to form the band that was to become Angel and the Brains.

At the end of 1964, with the blessing and the support of all their parents, they started to look for somewhere to practice.

"If we are going to play the type of music we like we need somewhere to practice where people won't complain about the noise," one of the boys said gloomily.

"My father has been working on this." Angelo told the boys. "You know the amusement arcade in Via Manlio Torquato? I know the owner from soccer and he has a basement that is not used. We are going to see him this afternoon."

The amusement arcade had been one of Angelo's

favourite places as a young boy where he enjoyed playing on the game machines. He remembered the friendly owner, Vincenzo, who had also been president of the local soccer club and encouraged him to play for the team. Although he enjoyed soccer very much, unfortunately, during the second game he played Angelo was injured. By the time he was fit enough to play again the demands of music and school were too much.

Angelo and his father visited him to ask if the boys could practice in the basement of the arcade. Vincenzo was only too happy to support the dedicated young band and happily allowed them to use it for free.

Angelo took the other band members to have a look at their new rehearsal place. The friendly owner greeted them warmly.

At this point there were only three in the band, two guitars and Angelo as the singer. The boys started to practice while they continued to look for a drummer, keyboard player and a bass guitar.

"What are you going to call yourselves?" asked Vincenzo. The boys looked at each other and back to Vincenzo, "We hadn't even thought about it!"

"Well I can't tell people about the great band in my

basement if they don't have a name!"

"Let us think about it and we'll get back to you" said Ruggero. Angelo told the others that it would be up to them to choose the name.

The boys tossed around names but nothing really appealed. To stop the debate Angelo said, "Well, I am angel, what are you?"

Again the boys couldn't come up with an answer. "You are a bright lot aren't you?" Angelo jokingly he added. "A bunch of real brains!"

The others stopped arguing and look at Angelo, then Maurizio, clicking his fingers, said, "That's good! Why not call us The Brains". They all agreed and went upstairs to Vincenzo's office. In almost perfect unison they announced. "The band you have in your basement is Angel and the Brains!"

A few days later when the boys were gathering together to practice, Maurizio brought in a short chunky boy and introduced him as Alberto, the keyboard player he had told them about.

Ruggero asked, "Alberto, what type of music do you like and what do you play?"

Alberto looked down at his feet, embarrassed to

tell these boys about his music training. "Well," he answered tentatively, "I study classical music. But," he added quickly, perhaps sensing their reactions, "I was tired of that and got myself an organ and I've started to play modern songs on that. I love that English band, the Beatles, and I play their music all the time."

"All of us know The Beatles and love their music. It is close to what we want to perform but with a different beat. Their music is British Beat, we want to create an Italian Beat but we still need a drummer and a bass player," Angelo explained.

Alberto was accepted as the new keyboard player and the next day he arrived at the basement with his organ.

The original Angel and the Brains band members were Angelo Ferrari (vocals), Ruggero Coletta (guitar), Alberto Del Duca (keyboard) and Maurizio Vitti (guitar). All the boys originated from Appio-Tuscolano, Rome, and all felt the same about traditional Italian music—that it was uninspiring for young people.

At that time Angelo's father was a Customs Inspector at Fiumicino Airport – Leonardo Davinci (Rome International).

As he was passing through the airport reception one

day he heard a voice calling, "Mr Ferrari, Mr Ferrari!" He turned to see one of the cleaners running towards him.

As she caught up to him she said breathlessly, "I heard that your son has a band and they are looking for a drummer".

"Yes, that is right," he replied. "Why? Do you know someone who might be interested?"

"Yes, my son Lino plays drums and is not too bad," she replied with a proud smile.

Angelo's father gave her the address of the basement and told her, "Tell Lino to be there any day around 10 in the morning. They are there every day at that time to start practising."

"You can tell your son to expect him," she replied.

Lino strolled in a week later ready to set up his drums. The boys looked at him, confused. Without even meeting them, he had brought his kit, as though his acceptance in the band was a given.

He must have realised the other boys were a bit taken aback and quickly said, "Hi, I'm Lino, I think I was expected. Angelo's father told me to come down. I brought my drums with me so you can hear my playing and tell me if I am good enough or not."

"You're right, sorry if we looked confused," said Ruggero.

"OK then, let's play something," grunted Alberto.

Well at least for the moment they had a drummer.

*Angel and the Brains from left Maurizio, , Alberto, Angelo, Enrico,*
*Ruggero and Lino*

Vincenzo, the arcade owner, was very supportive and knew they were looking for other musicians to join the band. People would say, "Oh you've got a band down there? They've got a great sound, wish I could play with them."

"Yes, they are looking for other musicians, why don't you talk to them?" he would encourage.

That's how they found their bass player, Enrico.

As they walked through the arcade on their way to practice one morning, they noticed the tall young man with short black hair playing on one of the machines and watching them as they went downstairs into the basement.

"Hi, my name is Enrico, the owner of the arcade told me you are looking for a bass player. I play the bass and I was looking for a band to join. Would you give me a try?"

"Sure," Angelo replied, "but do you have your own bass guitar and amplifier?"

"I have them at home." The young man replied eagerly. "I don't live far from here.  If you can give me half an hour I'll be back."

At 20, Enrico was a little older than the other boys but he fitted in well with the group and their music.

The word had spread through family and friends, and finally they had a drummer and bass player and the band was complete.

For several months the boys practised every day in the basement of the arcade, except for a month over the Christmas/New Year holidays. They performed songs of other artists but re-arranged them to suit their own style and were finally successful in getting bookings for six or seven shows in small towns. Although at this time they were only drawing small audiences, the boys and their new sound were well received.

Their repertoire included the most popular Italian songs of the time and some songs by the Shadows and The Beatles to give a wide variety.

Angelo told me, "All the songs were re-arranged to demonstrate what we were trying to achieve; create what we called an Italian beat. They had more rhythm and more sparkle to them and ultimately we had our own style. The drums were more prominent and bass guitar took away the symphonic sound that was in original arrangements. Put simply, there was more beat and no orchestra-like sound. The organ was only a backing not the main instrument as in the past."

In the summer of 1965 Angelo's aunt and uncle from Canada visited Italy for a holiday.
His cousin, Grace, would go to the basement to listen to the boys practice.

"You know, Ange, with your voice you would do really well in Canada and even the States. You've got the sort of voice they listen to there," she commented one day.

The basement had served very well as a place to practice. Vincenzo was very careful to make sure the boys were left alone to practice and that their instruments were safe from damage and theft.

If someone tried to open the door to the basement while the boys were practising he would stop them with a firm, "No you are not allowed down there."

At night, when he was closing up, he would make sure the door was locked before he left. It was not unlocked again until the boys picked up the key the next day.

While the boys were happy with the arrangement they had with Vincenzo they found the basement a bit dark and dingy. It was very limited in space when the six of them had to fit in with all the instruments. They were also very conscious that the music might be a bit loud for the people upstairs.

They mentioned this to Vincenzo who protested, "You can stay as long as you like!" But then shook his head and said sadly, "But you really do need a bigger place."

In need of a suitable new place to practice, Angelo's
father and the boys approached the monsignor of
Santa Maria Ausiliatrice, in the Tuscolano district of
Rome, and again not far from where the boys lived.
They told him about the band and asked if the boys
could use one of the big rooms at the side of the
cathedral. "You would be very welcome boys," the
monsignor told them.

*Santa Maria Ausiliatrice*

"We can't afford to pay for the hire," warned one
member of the group, mournfully.

"That's alright," said the monsignor, "we have an
empty room on the side of the Oratorium, it is not

used very much and you can practise there for nothing."

They moved all their gear to the Oratorium in October 1965.

Just before the move, the bass player, Enrico, was called up for military service. They needed to replace him quickly and decided to hold an audition. Being the only band in the area, it was a rare opportunity for ambitious, young, local musicians and six or seven hopefuls came along. A couple of them were not very good and Angelo told them they needed more practice.
However, there were a couple of very good players among them and it took some time for the boys to agree that Maurizio Aloisi should be the one to join them.

With their spacious new premises, all six band members could fit easily.

"Now we have room to breathe and light to see what we doing," smiled Lino.

"Hey guys, look over there! Is that a soccer table?" called Maurizio, prowling around the room and poking in its corners. The boys went closer to investigate and soon four of them were engrossed in a game, but it didn't take long before an indignant voice dragged them back to reality.

"Hoi! Are we here to practice or what?" shouted Lino.

"Come on, he's right," Ruggero urged.

Practice was every afternoon six days a week. That was the arrangement with the Monsignor because in the school next to the rehearsal room was full of students each morning until one p.m.

"It was probably six months from when we started the group to when we got our first gig," Angelo laughed, describing one concert in a nursing home for elderly people and how the band had had to adjust their music and put some of the old popular Italian songs in the repertoire. Staying true to their music though, they performed the songs in their own style.

"People were jumping up and down. Some of them in wheelchairs and some with walking sticks also tried to dance. It was great fun."

Angelo recalled other gigs were at prestigious restaurants in the small towns of Rocca Priora and Marino and a New Year's Eve concert on 31st December 1965 in another big restaurant.

Rock and roll had swept the United States and England like a tidal wave but for Italian teenagers, American music, especially the surfing sounds, were neither popular nor relevant. The Italian teenagers were more interested in English bands like The Beatles and the Mersey Beat sound.

The Beatles were part of the British Beat movement that had taken over the music scene in England and even invaded America from 1964. It provided the model for many important developments in pop and rock music.

It was known as Mersey Beat or Mersey Sound because of the hundreds of bands performing at dance halls in and around Merseyside, (the area around the Mersey River in Liverpool) the most famous being The Cavern Club where The Beatles were discovered.

Angelo explained, "As kids we picked up on the Beatles and from there figured out how it could be done—an Italian beat—and that's partly how the Mass became instrumental in the popularity of the Italian beat. You will read many sources crediting the Barrittas with the Italian Beat.

The Barrittas had nothing to do with the beat even for the Mass. The only beat there was the Bumpers and us—that's it!"

He went on to say, "The Beatles came out with songs that were very different in sound to the American rock and roll bands. Their new sound was not rock and roll and they never wrote rock and roll songs, they had their own unique music. While the Rolling Stones were closer to the American style they were not as popular as The Beatles in Italy."

Admiring The Beatles and their new sound, Angel and the Brains were finally able to refine their style. It was from there the Italian Beat started, which also became known as the 'putting beat' of Italy.

It was late January 1966, just over three months after moving their rehearsals to the cathedral Oratorium, that their future music career finally started to have a very positive direction.

"We didn't attend church on a regular basis but we had grown up with the Church being part of our lives and were all fairly good Catholics. We were just not into the religious side of things. The priests at the cathedral would scold us because we were practising there and never went to church.

This is why we were so surprised when maestro Giombini and some priests visited us one day.

"In the early part of 1966 we weren't angry with the church, we knew what the Catholic Church was all about because we grew up in Rome, but didn't really care."

# 4. Angel and the Brains meet Giombini

## *Pope John XXIII*

Pope John XXIII was born Angelo Roncalli. In 1953 he was created a cardinal and sent to Venice as Patriarch.

When Angelo was a little boy his family lived in Venice and his father knew Cardinal Roncalli well from when they travelled on the ferry together for years; Angelo's father going to work and the cardinal going to the cathedral each morning. During their morning chats he made it clear to Angelo's father that he thought the church needed shaking up.

*A Venetian ferry of the 1950s*

*Pope John XXIII*

Angelo met him on several occasions and found him to be very intelligent and very progressive in is his thinking and related some wonderful stories about him to me; stories both endearing and amusing. Throughout his church life he worked with his people and understood their needs.

Pope John XXIII had long experience and understood people's needs. He believed in plain speech and used everyday language and believed that the Catholic Church should be 'opening windows' and 'not museum-keepers but gardeners to help things grow'.

Pope John believed that modern society was witnessing a crisis as the world made great material progresses that were not always in keeping with Christian morals. He saw a world pursuing earthly pleasure and ignoring spiritual values.

He felt he had an urgent duty to call church leaders together to discuss the problems of the modern age and how the church could contribute to the solutions.

On 25th January 1959, less than three months after his election, Pope John gave notice of his intention to convene an Ecumenical Council.

This was the twenty-first Ecumenical Council of the Catholic Church, a conference of church dignitaries and religious experts brought together to discuss the doctrines and practices of the church.

The previous council, known as the First Vatican Council, had been held in 1868, so this one was called the Second Vatican Council and known informally as Vatican II.

He saw Vatican II as demonstrating that the Church was 'always living and always young, which feels the rhythm of the times and which in every century beautifies herself with new splendour, radiates new light, achieves new conquests'.

Vatican II was convened on 11th October 1962. One of the changes that Pope John XXIII wanted was to make the Church more relevant to the young people, to modernise the Church and be more welcoming to entice them to follow its spiritual path, rather than exhort them to do so.

Pope John XXIII died in June 1963, before he had been able to lead the Church through the reforms of Vatican II. Had he still been the hand on the tiller of the Catholic Church, things might have been very different today.

### *Giombini*

While the boys were getting their band together and perfecting their new sound, Marcello Giombini was making a name for himself writing movie soundtracks.

The young Giombini had been a church organist in Rome and pursued a music career. He became choir director for the Accademia Filarmonica Romana and was orchestra director for Orchestra Sinfonica di Roma until the 1950s.

His love of music led him to writing symphonies and conducting Renaissance music. The future would see Giombini's music compared to the great musicians and performers of the past, from Bach to Mozart,

Verdi to Perosi.

By the 1960s his long career writing successful movie soundtracks had already started, but it was to be his religious music that would bring worldwide notoriety.

Giombini was a luminary of contemporary music. He had written his first religious music, *Thou shalt not kill*, which was released by the Barrittas on 45 rpm record in 1965, with some success. However, Giombini went on to make a name among young Catholics in 1966 writing *La Messa dei Giovani (Mass for the Young)* which became known simply as *La Messa* or the *Beat Mass*. It was to become famous for its innovative liturgical music and for the resulting popularity of the Italian Beat sound.

### *Sinaldi*

One of the outcomes of Vatican II was a desire to make the church more appealing to young people. Monsignor Sinaldo Sinaldi, a Dominican priest whose order specialised working with young people, conceived the idea of holding a special mass based on modern music.

He was close to the world of cinemas, well-known movie critic, an influential member of the Catholic Centre Cinema and knew Giombini by reputation and as a composer of soundtracks.

He told Giombini about his idea to encourage young people to return to the church. It was certainly a daring initiative but Father Sinaldi's idea was not necessarily implausible.

Vatican II had stressed the need to 'admit to divine worship all forms of true art having the needed qualities'. Thousands of young people were attracted to popular music but were drifting away from the church.

Father Sinaldi thought that if 'beat' music could reach young people, then why not put it in a service of the Church?

Giombini was very enthusiastic about the concept and composed La Messa for voices, guitars, bass, keyboards and percussion. As the purpose of the Mass was to appeal to the young, it was deliberately composed to suit the new beat music.

He collaborated with Giuseppe Scoponi, Professor Tommaso Federici and Charles Gasbarri who wrote the words and finalised the work.

The Mass comprised nine songs: *Introit, Gloria, Gradual, Creed, Offertory, Sanctus, Pater Noster, Agnus Dei* and *Communio*.

The planned church service was not meant to be just a novelty event but a turning point, intended to make a mark in the profound liturgical music reform desired by the Vatican II.

Monsignor Sinaldi worked with Marcello Giombini on the presentation of the Mass. They already had two bands lined up to perform the work.

While telling the priests of Santa Maria Ausiliatrice about the plans for the Mass, Sinaldi mentioned that they still needed one more band that would be suitable. He was told about the young group of boys just starting out and using one of the rooms for practice. The priests believed they had enormous potential and would be ideal as the third band Sinaldi and Giombini were seeking.

### *Angel and the Brains Meet Giombini and Sinaldi*

In late January 1966 Sinaldi and Giombini went to the Santa Maria Ausiliatrice. They quietly entered the grounds from Via Don Rua and silently hid outside the door of the room where Angel and the Brains were practising.
The boys didn't see or hear them as they secretly listened to the band rehearsing.

It wasn't until the next day that Sinaldi and Giombini returned and introduced themselves, although it wasn't until later that the boys found out about their secret eavesdropping to determine if this band had that special something that the organisers were looking for.

"We have a proposition. We are organising a rock Mass and need another band to perform part of it. Are you interested in coming and performing for the Mass?" Giombini asked bluntly.

The boys stood in amazement as Giombini explained, "It will be held at the St. Filippo Neri Oratorium, Sala Borromini and there will be three groups there. We'd like you to be one of them." Two other bands, The Barrittas and The Bumpers, had already been signed.

Sinaldi outlined what he was hoping to achieve with the Mass. He explained that because it was an experiment, immediately after the performance he would lead a discussion on the success of the concept with those in attendance.

Expecting it to be a great success he also explained that before the Mass, the bands would be recording the songs for an album to be released the same day.

"Can you give us ten minutes to discuss it among ourselves please?" Angelo asked. Sinaldi and Giombini agreed to give the boys some time to discuss it.

"Take as long as you want. We'll wait outside. Just call us when you have made a decision," Giombini smiled knowing it probably wouldn't take the boys long.

As soon as their visitors departed, the boys started talking enthusiastically.

"I think we should take it," said Ruggero. "Why?" asked Lino. "Because it will give us the opportunity to be recognised as a professional band with a record out there," replied Ruggero.

"Yes but it would be religious music, we are trying to get our new beat sound out there," argued Maurizio.

"Religious music or not, we should take it, even just to get the recording studio contract. Then we'll see after the Mass what comes up," said Angelo.

Having personally known Pope John XXIII, his personal ambition to progress the Church and understanding the aims of Vatican II, Angelo was probably more enthusiastic than the other band members to participate in the Mass.

It was a great opportunity for the young band and all of them soon saw the advantages to them. As Giombini had forseen, their discussion didn't last long; they all agreed very quickly.

Ruggero invited Giombini and Sinaldi to come back inside.

"OK." Angelo told them. "We all agree. We will be very happy to do the Mass. How do we go about it?"

Giombini returned a week later with the sheet music and a recording of the music played by him on piano.

"Listen to the music I have played, but please put your own arrangement to it and we'll see what it is like," he told them. "I want each band to play in their own style and put their own personality to it."

After Giombini had left Angelo turned to the other boys excitedly, "Well, we don't know what the songs are like, but at least we can play them our own way!"

They listened to the tape Giombini had left, one song at the time, discussing each one as they went.

"OK this was the *Introito*," said Ruggero. "It is very slow we need to sparkle it up more."

"Yes it need little bit of beat in it," Maurizio agreed.

At the end of the second song Angelo said happily, "This is better, it has something we can really work with. It is faster and will be easy to put a good beat in it." They all concurred.

Finally they listened to the third song. It was good and very melodic but would be very difficult to add the beat to it. They decided to leave practising this song last.

The last song Giombini wanted the boys to learn and perform was not one they had to record.

The band practised even harder and more passionately than they had before, understanding that this was a great opportunity to make a big name for themselves, and that fame and acceptance was possibly within reach.

Every day brought new arguments born out of the desire to perfect their sound—arguments about a certain pass, the rhythm and even the notes— but they were united in the sound they wanted to achieve, and always managed to agree in the end.

Giombini called in to visit at least once a week to monitor progress, and liked what he heard.

Only  once or twice did he suggest a different way of doing something.

The boys worked hard and although they were ready within six weeks, they kept practising every day right up to the day before the performance.

## Recording the album

A few weeks before the big day the three promising bands Angel and the Brains, the Barrittas and the Bumpers recorded the songs for the album to be released the same day as the event.

This gave Angel and the Brains their first record contract with Ariel. In addition to the LP, Ariel also released a 45rpm record of them playing *Graduale (con voci di gioia)/Introito (penso pensieri di pace) [Gradual (with voice of joy)/Take (I think thoughts of peace)]*.

Angelo believed that the other song they had been given to perform, *Offertorio*, was a better song and is still disappointed that *Introito* was chosen.

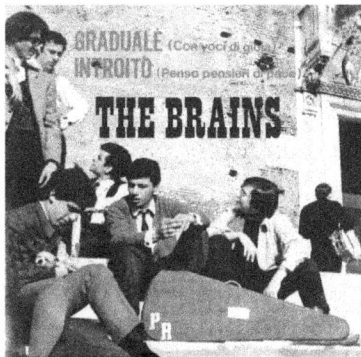

LA MESSA DEI GIOVANI

In the recording studio Angel and the Brains experienced some stressing days.

"When you're ready," the sound engineer would boom at them, startling them all.

The band would start and then suddenly, "Stop, no good, let's take it again!" would came the disembodied voice from the other side of the glass.

The band would start over again and then one of the members of the group would make a mistake.

"OK, stop and start again," they were told, and then, perhaps understanding their nerves, playing in a strange environment and recording their first-ever record, the engineer said kindly, "We'll get there, just relax guys."

Angel and the Brains were new to recording, but apart from the stress they found it to be an exciting experience. They worked four hours a day five days a week to get the recording completed in two weeks.

The songs had been rehearsed almost to perfection, the recording was completed, now all Angel and the Brains had to do was to wait for the day of the performance of the Mass. At this time, they still hadn't met the other bands and had no idea what their style was going to be like.

The inside cover of the album describes the music of each of the bands.

> *The Barrittas are already known to the public for their extensive discography and for the intense activity carried out in the premises of the capital and major Italian cities. The pieces placed in their execution (Gloria and Agnus Dei) lead a trademark of spontaneity and genuine musicality which we all now know and love.*

*The Bumpers (in their first experience in the recording field) have been prepared with the utmost seriousness for this difficult test. Their style, which closely follows the footsteps of the British beat processed and interpreted according to the sensitivity of the band, has already been brought to the attention of younger audiences. Their great versatility has allowed the production of enthralling and highly rhythmic parts as the Creed, the Sanctus and the Communio, and a song with a sweet and calm melody of the Pater Noster*

*Angel & the Brains are also new to the recording studio but they are not newcomers to the world of music. Each of them has a decade of musical training to his credit. The Mass has provided them with an excellent springboard and the opportunity to demonstrate their great possibilities. The interpretation Angel & the Brains have given the songs entrusted to their execution is proof of the results that can be achieved with the study together with a great passion for music.*

Professor Tommaso Federici, one of the Mass lyricists of the Pontifical Liturgical Institute, and Father Sinaldo Sinaldi invited the faithful to attend the *La Messa dei Giovani*, which was to be held just over half a kilometre from the Vatican itself.

# 5 The Mass

## *Promotion*

To promote the new concept, priests travelled around Rome putting up posters at most of the cathedrals and churches, and Father Sinaldi arranged for articles in some of the newspapers.

There was no allocated seating and it was a free event for people to just come along. Although everyone was hopeful of the concert having a positive impact, no-one had any idea how many people would turn up.

## *Angel and the Brains arrive and set up*

Angel and the Brains arrived at 4pm and everything was reasonably calm. Angelo noticed there were two police cars and four officers assigned to assist with crowd control if necessary. Their job was to keep people out of the building until the doors of the church were opened at five-thirty p.m.

He turned to the rest of the band members, "Let's go and see what we have to do. We can check the stage and have a chat to Giombini."

As they went inside they saw Giombini at the stage talking to Father Sinaldi and another priest. When they saw the boys they asked, "Hi boys, is everything alright?"

"Yes thank you, is there anything we need to know?" Angelo asked.

Giombini told them, "No, you know your songs and here is the order of songs for the performance. I don't need to tell you anything else; you know what you are doing. Father Sinaldi will show you where everything is."

He left to go into the office and the priest showed them where to set up their instruments. "If there is anything else we will let you know later. Just set up your instruments for now."

Alberto looked around the austere, empty Oratorium, again typical of Borromini's style, rectangular in shape but with rounded corners.

He looked up at the balconies and terraces, shuddered, then looked back at the stage where they had set up their instruments on the right hand side.

"At least it is a convenient place to be set up, we can escape if necessary. Look, the door to go outside is only five metres from where we will be performing," he joked nervously.

Angelo smiled to himself, "I think he is imagining himself at one of those concerts in the US or England that they show on TV with musicians needing to escape from the crowd!"

Angelo and Ruggero went outside. Maurizio and Alberto had gone across the road and came back with coffee for everyone. They sat drinking their coffee and smoking trying to calm their nerves.

Just before 5pm Angelo called to the others, "Let's go back inside and finish setting up."

As they went in he noticed a crowd growing outside and wondered what was happening. Surely all these people gathering couldn't be for them. *There must be someone famous coming*, he thought to himself. The crowd was so large he couldn't see the forecourt at all.

They noticed one of the other bands, The Barrittas, had already set up their gear that morning. As they started to put their equipment in place Father Sinaldi bustled up, and said, "Don't put your microphone there yet, The Bumpers will need to get past there to set up themselves."

The Bumpers arrived just as Angel and the Brains were almost finished setting up. Angelo remembers them as nice guys, very friendly and close to their own age. The Bumpers took no time to have everything in place and turned to Angel and Brains to introduce themselves.

"So, you are the kids that Giombini chose. You must be good; the maestro doesn't take just anyone, only those he thinks are the best. He knows what he's doing and has enormous experience."

Between the equipment of all three bands there were thousands of watts of amplification. After everything was set up by all the bands young Maurizio looked around in awe. He turned to the others "Wow, *Communio* is going to be tremendous."

The only other people in the Oratorium at that time was the technical crew from RAI setting up lights and cameras. Laughing, the band yelled into the mikes at them, "Can you hear us?"

## Crowd swells

There were no presold seats for the general public, but as the Oratorium could hold 2,000 people, organisers had believed there would be ample room. However, the crowd waiting outside for the doors to open started to swell to such a degree that the police had to call for reinforcements to control them. By five p.m. there were two police trucks, three vans and six cars.

The special guests, including priests representing nearly all levels of church hierarchy, had been seated half an hour beforehand and were the only ones guaranteed a place.

The first two rows were full of cardinals, bishops, priest, nuns and novices. The third row was filled with journalists and some politicians.

A reporter asked some of the people waiting to go in to explain the reason for their presence. "Well, yes, we are interested in the *Messa dei Giovani*," said a group of boys and girls, "but, more than anything, we came to listen to the bands."

An old lady said "I have not heard anything, but I'm sure the Church does not listen to this music ever!"

"I came to see with my own eyes," said an elderly, distinguished gentleman "how this kind of music can be applied to the sacred texts of the Mass. "

Another woman, in her fifties said, "After all, today's music is beautiful. I feel good that the young people, who I thought were just restless and wild, can think in this way to raise the level of their music."

While the band members were gathered in the courtyard waiting to start, he asked them how they felt about the Mass.

They replied, "We are convinced that beat music, the music of our time, is a valid form today as was Gregorian music in its time. When we were asked to play a 'Mass of the young', we were a bit confused but, after listening to the music and the lyrics, we realised that it is a very serious thing."

Summing up his interviews he wrote, 'We can say that a good half of the participants took it seriously'.

At one point Father Sinaldi picked up a microphone, "I ask the police to clear the yard. There is a window in danger." Five minutes later there came the sound of breaking glass, but fortunately it was just a lamp exploding.

At five-thirty p.m. the doors opened and the police struggled to control the entry.

"Stand back, all of you!" shouted a policeman, "let this lady and gentleman pass by first," referring to a couple in their 50s. This was a little ironic when the Mass had been designed to attract young people.

Nobody, including the priests, had expected anyone over 40 to turn up but there were several hundred people in their mid-40s and 50s and even some in their 60s and 70s.

The police's only option was to form a human barricade in front of the Oratorium's entrance so they could control the crowd better. It finally worked and they started slowly letting people in.

After 2,000 people filled the hall another 8,000 were left outside. These were mostly young people aged between 16 to 20 years old.

When they couldn't get inside they immediately starting shouting and threatening to cause trouble. A television producer from RAI calmed them down by announcing, "RAI will install some big speakers around the square so you can all still listen to the music."

That eased the situation up to a certain point and the RAI technicians worked quickly to ensure everything was set up before the Mass started.

Some of the young people were still not happy because they couldn't see the performers.

The more agile ones tried to climb up to the windows or to get into the court yard on the side of the building.

### The performance

At 6.30pm Father Sinaldi, opened the concert. "In a hard and merciless era like ours, a profane music can be useful in expressing religious sentiments— although I want to assure you that the promoters of this enterprise have absolutely no intention of putting light music into the church's official cult, that is, its worship," he said.

The outfits of the three bands ranged from Sardinian costumes of the Barrittas to the Bumpers' neat black and silver to the latest fashion trend from England worn by Angel and the Brains.

Angelo and the Brains were the youngest group of the three with an average age of 18. The Bumpers averaged about 20 and the Barrittas 24.

The passion and eagerness of the young people in attendance was overwhelming and they were not disappointed with the performance. They responded as many teenagers around the world responded to rock music.  Even though the venue was full to capacity it didn't stop them trying to dance in the metre-and-a-half space between the stage and the first row of seats, while the end of each song was greeted by cheers and whistles.

The songs of the Mass and the album were:

### *Introito (Penso pensieri di pace)*
### *Introduction (I think thoughts of peace)*
Performed by Angel & The Brains. Lyrics by Gasbarri.

This is the introduction to the Mass. It encourages people to think of peace and brotherhood and to connect with God. It is quiet gentle introduction to the Mass but the English beat influence can be heard particularly in the backing instruments.

### *Gloria (Gloria al Signore)*
### *Praise the Lord*
Performed by the Barrittas. Lyrics by Scoponi

This song is a dedicated to the glorification of God. The tempo builds a little on the introduction but this band does not feature the drums and bass guitar like the Bumpers and Angel and the Brains.
It is the other instruments that are more prominent. There is a section in the middle that is very reminiscent of a Gregorian chant.

### Graduale (Con voci di gioia)
### Gradual (With joyful voices!)

Performed by Angel & The Brains. Lyrics by Federici.

Promoting singing a joyous Hallelujah to God, this song has a definitive Italian Beat. There are strong drums with a distinctive beat. Listening to this in 2013 it was very easy to imagine the teenagers bopping their heads finding it hard to resist getting up to dance.

### Credo (Io credo)
### I believe (I believe)

Performed by The Bumpers. Lyrics by Scoponi

The words here tell the people to believe in God, all the Saints, Jesus and Mary. You can hear a distinctive Merseybeat influence but there is no big bang on the drums.

### Offertorio (A te offro mio Dio)
### Offertory (To you I offer my God)

Performed by Angel & The Brains. Lyrics by Federici.

As this title says, it is an offering, an offering of the mind and soul to God on earth and in heaven. This is Angelo's personal favourite from the Mass and while it is a gentle song it has strong drums and guitar.
It best demonstrates what Angel and the Brains were trying to achieve in their music with the keyboard playing a background role and the emphasis on the beat provided by the drums and bass guitar.

### Sanctus (Santo)
### Holy (Holy)

Performed by The Bumpers. Lyrics by – Scoponi

The words praise God as the supreme Holy entity. The music does that in a very happy joyful way. There is excellent harmony in the voices and the joyfulness of it makes you want to move with the beat of the drums.

### Pater Noster (Tu che sei nei cieli)
### Pater Noster (Thou who are in heaven]

Performed by The Bumpers.  Lyrics by Gasbarri.

This is an adaption of the traditional Pater Noster – Our Father in heaven, Thy will be done.  It is performed as a ballad and retains a religious sound.

### Agnus Dei (Agnello di Dio)
### Agnus Dei (Lamb of God)

Performed by Barrittas. Lyrics by Scoponi.

This song praises Jesus as son of God that was crucified and prays to God to intervene on our behalf. It is very slow and quiet with the drums softly in the background. There is no strong beat.

### Communio (Rendete grazie a Dio)
### Communio (Give thanks to God)

Performed by all three bands. Lyrics by Scoponi

This is thanks to God and receiving his body in the form of bread. The Bumpers had recorded this song for the album but was performed together by all three bands at the Mass.

The bands had not had time to practice together and when it came to performing Communio they were all nervous but excited. It was agreed that because the Bumpers already knew the song and had recorded it, the other two would follow the Bumpers' arrangement.

To reduce mistakes, Angel and the Brains' drummer and rhythm guitarist, and the Barrittas' bass player and keyboard player did not actually play but mimed to give the appearance that they were. Angelo and the lead singer of the Barrittas took their lead from the Bumpers' vocalist.

In spite of the nerves and no rehearsal, the sound was loud but crisp and clear as it filled the Oratorium. Angelo recalls, "On stage it sounded like all the musicians in the world were playing together at the same time. It was incredible and exiting. We were grinning at each other and dancing around as we sang. "

While listening to the record in 2013, with its slight echo introduced to simulate what it would sound like in the lofty spaces of a church, I tried to imagine what is must have been like that day, particularly towards the end. The second-last song performed was a lovely slow, quiet song of praise then bang! Three bands giving thanks to God with volume and passion.

Is this all that remained in the critics minds? The descriptions of the songs show that they were holy songs, no different to the sentiments of church songs the world over. Could the problem then have simply been the volume and beat to which they were played?

Overall the reactions of the audience were quite varied from the ecstatic enthusiasm of the young people to elderly ladies praying with their rosaries held between their fingers. At the end of each track there was long applause, even by priests, and repeated calls for an encore.

A newspaper of the time described the anticipation:

> *The saints of the frescos at 6.30pm watched and listened for the first chords to shake them, the relentless pounding of the drums, interrupted only occasionally by a rapid cascade of notes by the electric organ, while the public (except the priests and the elderly) began to clap and move their heads rhythmically.*

One shocked lady was reported as saying, "But do you realise that five hundred meters from here there is the Pope?"

"It's a shame," thundered a big commander, "one should not allow things like that!"

Young people overhearing these comments yelled back, "It is always the same with the oldies. You haven't figured out that times have changed. At least we are not hypocrites; the songs are calling for peace and tell us not go to church with war in our heart."

With this range of opinions and reactions, it is not surprising that the debate following the Mass was very lively.

*Sala Borromini with the three bands*

# 6. Religious music causes an outcry

*Discussion following the Mass*

At the conclusion of the performance the bands stayed on stage while they waited for Father Sinaldi to join them and lead the discussion on the results of the experiment.

It didn't go according to plan. Before Father Sinaldi could reach the stage and pick up a microphone, a vocal explosion erupted inside the Oratorium.

A considerable part of the debate was based on the music's relevance and place in liturgy, that is its place in the actual rites of a Mass.

The debate that was to rage for years—and still does today—started with one student asking, "How can this music become part of the liturgical music?"

A friend of one of the bands responded, "This is not sacred music. You have to experiment with what spirit the youth of today can approach the liturgy."

Father Sinaldi as moderator, added, "Of course we must not judge the intentions, but the results. If this music is artistic, fine. That's what counts. On the other hand the music is defined as religious, but not sacred or liturgical."

This comment by the father was a direct reference to Vatican II stressing the need to 'admit to divine worship all forms of true art having the needed qualities'.

The comments, questions, points of view and arguments put forward were widely varied. Even the priests themselves were divided.

Some of the young people who spoke appeared better prepared than their older opponents.

One opinion on the negative reviews was that they were a knee-jerk reaction to the over enthusiasm of the young spectators with their thunderous applause and whistles of approval.

There was even a racist, inevitably present at all these events, who snatched the microphone from the hands of Father Sinaldi, to cry out, "We're not in Africa! It is devil's music."

And so the debate continued as priests close to the stage shuddered, a thousand questions on their tongues.

Maestro and priest Father Belli, Director of the Augustinian, tried to explain the basic principles of religious and liturgical music but was drowned out by the many conflicting views.

In reply to the young people claiming they had the right to worship in their own way, he stated, "There is no Mass without liturgy".

"But there are Masses not dedicated to the celebration of the rite," countered Sinaldi.

Belli argued, "It is not true. They were all written for the purpose of the liturgy. Only the concerts are not performed in church for the difficulties of the execution. But Verdi's Requiem, for example, was carried into the church".

Father Sinaldi asked, "Have you finished?"

Father Belli replied, "No, I asked if this music has a liturgical perspective. You answered 'no' and I am convinced. Then you say it is only religious. So I say, don't the words make any music religious or sacred? This music does not invite your reminiscence and meditation, but teases and does not dig into the soul".

"It is about praising God with happy music and happy thoughts" shouted a young man from the back.

Applause and interjection erupted from various quarters. From the young people who were in favour of the beat Mass, to Father Lopez Calo, commentator of Radio Vatican, who was against the Mass and back across the spectrum to Father Marsili, president of the liturgical San Anselmo, who supported it.

Father Sinaldi declared that he was satisfied that the Mass had been a success and this was evidenced by the participation and enthusiasm of the young.

Prior to the debate, Father Gino Bono had told a newspaper reporter, "I think the work is neither blasphemous nor disrespectful. Moreover, the texts of the songs are literary translations from the Latin Mass of the steps. It's just a form of attracting young people to the Church. Naturally, it is not a true Mass. We must make a distinction between religious music and sacred music. Before arriving to perform this music in the church, we must wait a whole series of consensus. Do not forget that we are in Rome, the centre of the Catholic Church."

What wasn't made clear was if the outcome of the consensus was against the experiment, particularly as it was in Rome 'the centre of the Catholic Church' that the Vatican would use interference and obstruction as a means to wipe it out.

### *In the news*

The next day one newspaper described the scene:

> *After enjoying the unique rhythms of Gloria, Gradual, Introit, Creed, Offertory, Sanctus, Pater*

*Noster, Agnus Dei and Communio, played and shouted with the same epidermal sensuality of the most modern songs of rebellion and love, Father Sinaldi, brandishing a microphone had to repeatedly scold his young friends that with screams and whistles, boxing match style, were clamouring with loud voices for a repetition of some of the music.*

Another article said:

*In the course of the debate, as was easily predictable, many questions arose. The same priests present were deployed in two opposing factions, pros and cons. The controversies have been many, and many more will arise. The good news is that the 'Mass of the Young' has affected everyone there, regardless of their approval or not. On the other hand the atmosphere in the Borrominian Hall, at the end of execution was too 'electric' for the debate to take place normally.*

# Messa «yé-yé» a San Filippo Neri

**Il singolare esperimento liturgico ha avuto per protagonisti tre complessi jazz · Le reazioni del pubblico**

*Il Temp headline 28th April 1966*
*English Translation: With guitars and hippies*
*Ye-ye Mass at St. Philip Neri The singular liturgical*
*experiment was to feature three jazz bands- The*
*reactions of the public*

# Continuano le polemiche sulla "Messa dei giovani„

Numerose lettere pervenute al nostro giornale - Alle precisazioni di padre Sinaldi, organizzatore del concerto, fanno riscontro le proteste di alti prelati

*Il Temp headline 4th May 1966*
*English Translation: Continue the controversy over the*
*Mass of the young people*
*Numerous letters have been received by our newspaper*
*– At the clarifications of Father Sinaldi, organizer of*
*the concert, counterpart the protests of other prelates*

The controversial debate continued in the newspapers with Il Tempo on 4th May reporting they received many letters on the subject. When they interviewed Father Sinaldi about the criticism of the Mass, Sinaldi pointed out that the debate had been recorded on tape and it was well documented that the majority of people were in favour of the initiative, as was most of the press. He cited Padre Marsili, head of the Pontifical Liturgical Institute, who expressed himself 'very favourable'.

I wonder where that tape is now. It would be very interesting to review.

However, Monsignor Domenico Celada, domestic prelate of His Holiness and Director of the magazine Pontifical Musical Chapel, referred to the Mass as a 'deplorable event in the Oratory of St. Philip Neri'.

When questioned about his response to the articles in newspapers reporting the debate, Angelo's reply was, "I don't know how the newspapers understood what was being said during the debate. All I recall was everyone screaming at each other."

Scanning the newspapers the day following the Mass the boys found other articles and were astounded at the reports of the Mass and not just the debate.

"Look at this," Alberto called to the others and read aloud from *Il Messaggero*, "'Never before has there ever been seen such a crowd, unleashing punches and kicks, assaulting a barred door, just to be able to assist at a Mass.'"

"Yes, it's the same in *Il Tempo*," said Angelo.

"What about this?" asked Ruggero. "The *Unita* says that so many people came to the Sala Borromini that the police had their hands full and even had to deal with a bunch of young people climbing the wall in the adjacent courtyard where there was a risk that a window could fall!"

"I didn't realise all that was going on outside," Alberto remarked, possibly disappointed to have missed all that excitement.

A few days later Maurizio Vitti tells them that his sister, who was a tour hostess, picked up articles in three newspapers from overseas.

"*The Times* newspaper from Idaho and the daily news from the Virgin Islands have called us 'mop-haired youths', and the paper from Oklahoma call us 'beatniks jamming at a Roman Mass'," he tells them.

# Beat Mass Draws Crowds To Church

ROME (AP)—Three mop-haired youth combos banged out a "beat mass" in a Roman Catholic chapel one night recently, and listeners couldn't agree whether it was a howling success or a holy mess.

A crowd of 500, including scores of priests, jammed into the oratory of St. Philip Neri. They stomped their feet and bobbed their heads to the rhythm of the electric guitars, drums, organ and singers.

Another 1,000 outside beat on the door trying to get in. Police reinforcements had to squeeze into the crowded courtyard to keep order.

A group of Oratorian fathers, whose religious order specializes in youth work, sponsored the mass.

The 17 young musicians were lined up before a battery of microphones to perform a nine-part mass written by composer Marcello Giombini, with words adapted by an editor of the Vatican newspaper L'Osservatore Romano, the Rev. Carlo Gasbarri. There was no religious celebration of the mass.

The Rev. Senaldo Sinaldi, a Dominican priest, opened the concert with this explanation:

"In a hard and merciless era like ours, a profane music can be useful in expressing religious sentiments—although I want to assure you that the promoters of this enterprise have absolutely no intention of putting light music into the church's official cult, that is, its worship."

The first combo, "Angel and the Brains," took off with a driving rendition.

"The Bumpers" took over when the first group stopped, and then "The Berets" took their turn.

On they raged through the introit, gloria, credo, sanctus and pater noster.

All three combos played and sang together in a climactic crescendo.

The Rome newspaper Il Messaggero commented:

"Never before has there ever been seen such a crowd, unleashing punches and kicks, assaulting a barred door just to be able to assist at a mass."

"They also say that the people there 'stomped their feet and bobbed their heads to the rhythm of the electric guitars, drums, organ and singers.'"

It went on to describe the scene:

> ... *the 17 young musicians were lined up before a battery of microphones to perform a nine part Mass written by composer Marcello Giombini, with words adapted by an editor of the Vatican newspaper L'Osservatore Romano, the Rev Carlo Gasbarri. There was no religious celebration of the Mass.*

"Look," said Angelo, "It has gone to those papers through a newswire service. They all use the same sentence: 'Listeners couldn't agree whether it was a howling success or a holy mess'.

"And only one of them talks about the last song when we all performed together. What a fantastic experience that was!"

# 7. Vatican reform or Vatican retreat

### *Before start of Vatican II*

Bishop Christopher Butler was intensely loyal to the church but considered the Vatican to be a 'colossus bestriding the world'. When he first heard that the Council had been called he wrote, "I feared another dose of authoritarian obscurantism."

Again, before the commencement of Vatican II he wrote, "What matters in the end is the successful achievement of the Council's intentions." Further, he expressed concern that if it was not achieved the church would become more irrelevant. Time has demonstrated how right the bishop was in his apprehensions.

During the opening Vatican II Pope John XXIII stated, "The Church should never depart from the sacred treasure of truth inherited from the Fathers. But at the same time she must ever look to the present, to the new conditions and the new forms of life introduced into the modern world. "

*Second Vatican Council*

### Aggiornamento

In his book published shortly after the Council had ended, Bishop Christopher Butler recalled his feelings at the time:

> So there was to be a Second Vatican Council. What would be its business? Nothing in particular, it would appear; or perhaps it would be truer to say: everything. ... Christian unity was the Pope's distant goal, no doubt, but his immediate aim was 'to let some fresh air into the Church' and to promote within her an *aggiornamento*.

Translated from the Italian *aggiornamento* means 'updating'.

Pope John XXIII had recognised that the Catholic Church was insular and that little had changed for over 400 years. After Vatican II, there was increased hope that the church would finally become more open minded.

Unfortunately he was unable to see his reforms to fruition and died in 1963.

Speaking after the close of the Council on 23rd April 1966, and only four days before the Beat Mass, Pope Paul VI stated, "Whatever were our opinions about the Council's various doctrines before its conclusions were promulgated, today our adherence to the decisions of the Council must be whole hearted and without reserve; it must be willing and prepared to give them the service of our thought, action and conduct. The Council was something very new: not all were prepared to understand and accept it. But now the conciliar doctrine must be seen as belonging to the magisterium of the Church and, indeed, be attributed to the breath of the Holy Spirit."

Another papal comment that referred back to the Council was John-Paul II who wrote on the eve of the new Millennium, "...there [in the Council] we find a sure compass by which to take our bearings in the century now beginning."

In his book published in 1968, just two years after the Mass, Bishop Butler states:

> *But— and here is the vital point at which the Council becomes a challenge to us all— the Acts of the Council are, in and by themselves, historical documents already dead when the conciliar fathers were at last dismissed. If the Council was, and I argue that it was indeed, potentially a new Pentecost, it will only prove to have been actually such if the Church now goes on to live the Council. This, of course, it has begun to do; but how insufficiently up to this date. The very texts of the documents have, so far, been only very imperfectly communicated, expounded, understood and assimilated. But there is more, much more, to the Second Vatican Council than the letter of the texts subscribed by its members. The Council substituted the dynamic for the static as the appropriate category for Christian thinking and acting.*

### Forty Years On—Urgency of Aggiornamento Underlined

Despite many articles in both print and on the internet covering the purpose and outcomes of

Vatican II, little seems to have changed, and the admirable aims of the Council seem to have been lost somewhere.

The Vatican II—Voice of the Church website describes how Bishop Butler 'became increasingly concerned about the slow pace of implementation'.

The material about and by Butler on the website is intended to lead a newcomer into Butler's work, but he endorsed the view that it is far more important is to use his work to stress the ongoing relevance of the Vatican II, as emphasised by successive popes.

### Lost with aging men

There has been some progress in some areas, particularly in relation to the language used in a Mass and conciliation with other religions, but other reforms have not eventuated.

Many writings, including several from within the church, express concern that the Vatican today is ignoring, or distorting Council teaching.

Today there is disquiet that, even within the Catholic Church, as time goes on the legacy of Vatican II is being lost and those that are openly positive about the Council's progressive aims are viewed with some suspicion.

Many original teachings are becoming obscured partly because there is now limited living memory of the Council and because elements in the Vatican seem to be imposing one-sided interpretations of both Council texts and of the fathers' intentions. It must be asked: can important questions be closed unilaterally while remaining reasonably disputed?

Archbishop Denis Hurley OMI also expressed concern that with time the intentions of Vatican II are being forgotten 'there are fewer and fewer Catholics who can remember [Vatican II] when the Church took a giant step forward.... and what a terrible loss that is proving to be'.

Communication about the debates within the Council was poorly handled with no clear explanations and the people both inside the church and among the general population have had to rely on press reports. When changes to the liturgy were made, for example, they were not explained satisfactorily to the people, but were simply put into place.

### *Inspired by Vatican II*

The creation of the beat Mass had drawn its inspiration based on the outcomes of Vatican II and innovations being introduced into the Catholic Church.

When Pope John XXIII ascended to the papal throne after the death of Pius XII (1958) he expressed concern that there was a gradual move away from the Church, especially by young people, and believed the Church needed to 'open their arms to the people'. This led to the work of Vatican Council II (1962–1965).

In the May 1965 edition of the *Rocca* magazine, Jesuit Father Pedro Arrupe wrote:

> *In the young there is a lot of dynamism and especially a lot of sincerity. They appear sometimes hostile to religion but are just intolerant of formalisms and exteriorisation of the faith.*

This quotation was also used on the inside cover of the album.

### *Music critics*

The church had stressed the need to 'admit to divine worship all forms of true art having the needed qualities'.

Father Sinaldi had declared during the debate, "If this music is artistic, fine. That's what counts."

While the young Catholics loved the music of the master for the liveliness of its sound and insightful lyrics, Giombini himself also came in for criticism about his music, which he seemed to take with equanimity.

Giombini said the critics were honest in their criticism and their reaction was justifiable because the Mass could have been interpreted as an affront to the way that sacred music was conceived. He explained it had not been his intention to cause conflict and he had created a different way of singing that was closer to the young people because the council of the Vatican had stated that it wanted the church to progress forward.

Giombini had even came up with a slogan he wanted to use, but couldn't after all the controversy. The slogan was 'pick up the guitar and pray', because the guitar for the young people at that time represented their way of expression.

Most of the critics of the music written for the Mass, including organists and choir directors, were traditionalists. They said the compositions were not suitable for meditation and prayer and quite inappropriate to the solemnity of church rituals. The harshest critics claimed Giombini's film scores were very poor and, during a conference in Mexico, Giombini was even accused of being an atheist.

Valentino Miserachs Grau, former head of the Pontifical Institute of Sacred Music and Director of the Liberian Musical Chapel claimed that 'the noises' were uninspiring and temporary. He called them, "Unscrupulous merchants, that have dried up the pure sources of Gregorian chant and of cultured popular music that constitute the most beautiful decoration of our churches and celebrations while provoking a hateful undisputed malignant environment, because it occurs within the Church and against the Church itself."

The aftermath was also described as having the effect of a nuclear meltdown, with critics accusing it as being mass-market music, inconsistent, insipid and short-lived. It was also wrongly and unjustly referred to as popular, disconcerting, clamorous and noisy with twisted manifestations that delighted huge, undiscerning crowds at what were erroneously called 'concerts'.

Giombini loved the fact that none of his critics actually assessed his songs for the way they brought joy to many young people who saw this way of singing as their path to the glory of God.

The new beat sound was soon replaced in both liturgical music and in its status in the more mainstream popular music, but discussion about the

Mass of the Young would be proven to be far from simple and short lived. It was in fact a turning point in profound liturgical music, which would never be the same again.

The music, which had been intended to accompany the congregation singing, went through great upheavals. It was poorly tolerated by traditionalists and unavoidably compared to Gregorian music.

### *Meeting the aims of Vatican II*

The Mass provided a momentum for the evolution of liturgical chant, believed at the time to be the aim of the innovative decisions of Vatican II. However, despite several attempts to bring this form of music back into the church, it has not been until more recent times that churches frequently include this form of music in church services.

The Catholic Church must have been well aware of the plans for the Mass. Giombini and Sinaldi had developed the concept for the Mass in 1965 after the aims of Vatican II were made public, as a way of fulfilling the aims of Vatican II. The Pope and the cardinals understood the idea, and it is almost certain that the subject would have been raised in discussion at the Vatican.

*La Messa dei Giovani*, organised by Father Sinaldi and other members of the Oratory of St Philip Neri, created by maestro Marcello Giombini, with words written by officials of the church and performed by the three young bands, had immediately caused a furore.

But this furore only marked the beginning of the arguments that would surround the controversial subject from the time the Church began to abandon the old forms of liturgical music to this day.

Angelo believes that the Vatican didn't understand the type of music that was proposed, but that the officials were content to let the Mass go ahead and simply wait and see what debate ensued.

And wait and see they did. Once they realised that some publicity was stridently against the idea of the Beat Mass and its *aggiornamento*, they turned on those that could not stand up against them.

## 8. Exciting outcomes

### *Move to theatre*

The priest who had baptised Angelo was the monsignor of the Santa Croce in Gerusalemme Cathedral and had told Angel and the Brains prior to the Mass that the theatre attached to his church was no longer used and they could use it for practise.

They had been so busy with practise, recording the records and the photo shoots for the Mass they hadn't had time to take him up on his offer. As soon as the Mass and its debate finished they packed up their instruments and amplifiers and took them straight to the new venue.

Being in the theatre helped them to improve their music. For the first time they were able to practise on a stage and with no school next door, they were no longer restricted to just practising in the afternoons.

The cathedral is one of the oldest in Rome and, at the time, it was basically as it was originally built, but the theatre had excellent natural acoustics.

"This is really good," declared Maurizio as they entered the theatre, gazing around in wonder.

"Yes, we can rehearse like we are performing in a

concert," Angelo agreed.

Ruggero wanted to know more about the acoustics and said, "We will need to check the sound as well, we only checked at the Mass but that was a church and the acoustics are different here."

"We will need to play something while you, Angelo, go down there and check the volume of all the instruments and we will adjust them accordingly," Alberto instructed.

With a new perspective on sound and acoustics, they were constantly trying new things. One of them would sit in the middle of the seating and listen to how the music sounded.

Oblivious to the seriousness of the arguments about the Mass that were raging, the young band members of Angel of the Brains had become an overnight success.

The great success of the Beat Mass aroused great attention around the world and the three bands were in demand from every quarter of the globe to recreate it.

### World Tour

On the Monday after the Mass Giombini visited the boys with exciting news.

"Looks like we are going to do a world tour of the Mass in Europe later this year and America and Japan early next year!"

The other members were busy tuning instruments and had not heard Giombini's news. Angelo called them over eager for them to hear.

The boys could not contain their elation at the thought of world travel and started jumping around.

"There is nothing definite in place yet," Giombini warned them, "but I hear it will be in some very prestigious venues."

"Wow! Do you think we'll get to the States?" asked Ruggero. "It is quite possible," smiled Giombini.

Giombini went on to tell them there would be extra songs to perform but didn't explain exactly what the songs would be, only saying that he was still writing them.

The boys were excited about the prospect of a tour but hoped the songs would be something different and not religious ones.

They were still developing their Italian beat sound with new songs and were hoping to have some of the songs recorded in English for the European and American market.

To their disappointment, they later discovered that the songs were to have religious themes.

"Well," said Ruggero philosophically, "at least we are going on a tour. We can still work on our music while we are away and see what happens after that."

Except for Angelo, who had visited some of the adjoining European countries, none of the boys had ever travelled outside Italy.

"Just imagine," enthused Maurizio, "being paid to sing and see the world!"

A month later the promoters in the UK, Belgium, France and Denmark were all on board.

The world tour was planned for September 1966 with bookings starting in the most prestigious venues. One was the Royal Albert Hall in London and others included venues of equal status in Belgium, Holland, the Scandinavian countries, Japan, France and even Broadway, concluding at the Olympia in Paris.

### *Concerts after the Mass and Angelo becomes the band's drummer*

The Mass, particularly with its extensive media coverage, had given Angel and the Brains a boost in popularity and being in demand, bookings for concerts soon started to come in.

The band had suffered a setback, however, immediately following the Mass with the departure of the drummer, who had moved to the south of Italy for a new job and was unable to continue with them.

With other drummers in the area still wedded to what the boys firmly called the 'old style', there was no drummer around who could produce the required beat. And without a drummer, the crisp and lively music produced by Angel and the Brains was full of gaps and sounded incomplete.

Unable to produce their trademarked sound, the band was disconsolate.

"What will we do now without a drummer?" Alberto wailed.

"There's only one thing for it," said Angelo. "I'll play the drums."

"But you're our singer," exclaimed Maurizio. "You can't do both!"

"I'll manage," replied Angelo confidently. He had already had some practice at the drum kit, having filled in on occasions when the drummer had been unable to make rehearsals. From the first time he sat at the drums he knew instinctively how to play and loved it. But not only was this an opportunity to play an instrument that he enjoyed, it gave him the opportunity to finally complete the sound for the band he had wanted all along.

He adamantly believed that the most important component of their new beat sound depended on having the right drumming style. At last he had the drumming style he wanted backing him—by creating and playing it himself.

Determined to have a constant beat with no gaps in the music, Angelo came up with a drumming style that others tried to copy and which he simply describes as 'filling in the gaps'.

(Even today in 2013 when I say to him, "I love this song, what do you think?" Nine times out of ten the response is, "Listen! The drummer isn't filling in the gaps!")

It was not uncommon for members of other bands to approach him following a performance to ask how he did it This included famous singers who had their own orchestra and the drummer, Mike (Micky) Wilding from the then popular and successful British group The Primitives.

The well-known and very popular Piper Club in Rome had three bands perform every night for a week. This was a regular activity for the club that seated 5,000 people. On one occasion Angel and the Brains played alongside The Camaleonti, one of the biggest names in Italy at the time, and the Primitives.

At the end of the week the club asked patrons to vote on the best band.

"I couldn't believe my ears when it was announced that we had won. My astonishment was because we were a new band against two of the best in bands in Europe," Angelo said.

Angelo admired and liked the band members of the Primitives. He remembers them as being professional, excellent musicians and very friendly despite being better known than Angel and the Brains. They showed no ill feeling about being beaten, congratulating Angel and the Brains on their win and shaking their hands.

Angelo also regretted that, because he didn't speak English and they only spoke a few words in Italian, communication was very limited.

Mike asked Angelo in a very broken Italian, "You do some passes on the drum that I would like to do myself."

"When we play next, stay next to me and tell me what

you mean," Angelo didn't clearly understand what Mike was talking about.

Each band played for about 45 minutes three times every night. Angel and the Brains started their next session on stage and Mike stood near Angelo. At one point he leant closer to Angelo and softly said in English "That...that's what I mean....how is done?"

"This is what I call filling the gaps. I'll show you." He did it a few times and Mike watched closely. At the end he said "I've got it.....I think. I'll try next time we go on."

Mike was a very good drummer and when they went on for their session he tried the technique and managed it immediately.

Angelo told me, "That's what I call a drummer. He is one with his instrument. He gave it a try and got it in one."

Angelo had created a new way of playing drums that gave more beat and created more interest musically. It took off around the world but, even today, many drummers can't emulate or are not successful in copying his style.

For five months (May to September) the band was in demand. They were driving like maniacs from Sicily up to the north of Italy performing in eight to ten concerts in cities and small towns every month with audience of 10,000 to 30,000 people at every concert.

Summers in the 1960s featured a festival or celebration of the town Saint in every city, town and village in Italy. Among the bookings the band received, many were for an appearance at these events.

The events were always on the weekend and often the band had to move quickly from one town to another, performing on a Saturday night in one place and the Sunday night in another.

More than once this involved driving more than 400 km on mountain roads to reach the next town by lunch time.

Often they didn't have much sleep but that was okay; they were young and these were exciting times.

Their new-found fame meant in the smaller towns and villages they were often the main attraction and instead of supporting other entertainers, they were themselves now supported by unknown or small-name performers. In the bigger towns and cities there were always two or three main attractions, but again supported by lesser-known artists.

The time was an eye opener to the entertainment business for the relatively naïve boys.

Right from the beginning they were astonished to see some of the big-name entertainers arguing about who should be last on stage so they could be acknowledged as the top artist.

The band never argued about it. They were just happy to be there and performing their music. Whether they were last or second last, generally it did not worry them. This only became an issue involving the band on one occasion when they had been listed as the top billing artist but another performer objected.

Angelo recalled the occasion, "It was one of the biggest stages we had performed on. It was enormous, with canopies at the back to make dressing rooms for the artists and a big open area behind the stage. It was in this open area that the incident happened."

The promoter had told the boys that a very well-known female singer had heard about them and would like to meet them.

She sashayed up to them, saying almost perfunctorily, "Hello boys, it's nice to meet you," before continuing with, "You know that I am going on last. I always go on last."

Angelo recalled that she was in her mid-30s and so stuck up she reminded him of some diva or an American movie star. Trying not to laugh, Angelo said it was alright for her to go on last, the band didn't mind.

The promoter, however, had returned just in time to hear this and protested immediately, "No! Sorry, but people here came especially to see and hear Angel and the Brains, the band that did the first Beat Mass in the world, so I need them to go on last." He turned to the band "Thank you for your understanding, but she has to go on before you."

The famous singer did not appreciate it at all that. Turning on heels she stormed away shouting, "I never! This has never happened to me before! This is the last time I will come to this town. There is really no respect......!" the rest of her tirade faded as she stamped off.

Angelo turned to the promoter, aghast. "Are you sure about this? She is upset now and she said won't come back to this town again. We really don't mind where we perform on the list."

"I don't give a damn!" snapped the promoter. "She's never going to perform in this town again? Well, I am going to tell her she is not going to do another show with me again!"

Angelo never knew what ultimately transpired between the singer and the promoter but she went on second last and they appeared last.

Because the concerts were nearly always on weekends, it gave the band time to head back to the recording studio during the week, so in between racing up and down the country performing, they recorded four more records.

In mid-May they recorded two more religious songs, *San Francesco (St Francis)* and *Volgi lo sguardo a me (Look down at me)*. Because the Mass was not long enough in itself for a concert, it was expected that these two songs would be included in the first part of the concert tour.

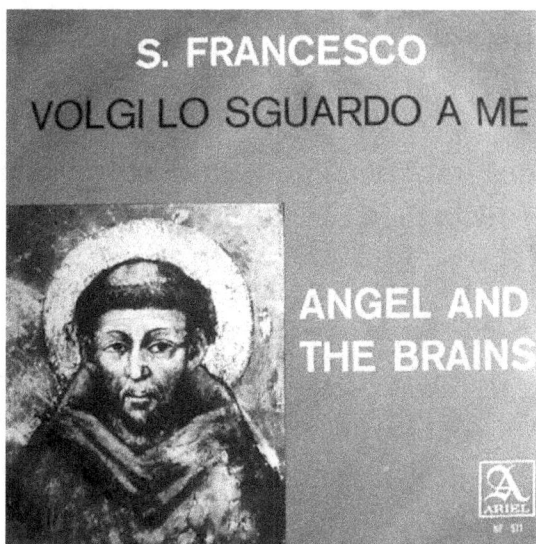

In June they recorded a track for the Italian comedy western *I due figli di Ringo (Ringo's Two Sons)*, in July another movie soundtrack *Le due Monachine* and in August *When You Went Away*, finally a song in English, for the spy movie *Blueprint for a Massacre*.

### Announcement of world tour

The headline read:

## For the First Time Three Italian Groups in the Home of the Beatles and Rolling Stones

The article in *Ciao Amici* announced that the Barrittas, the Bumpers and Angel and the Brains would perform *La Messa dei Giovani* at the Royal Albert Hall on 11th September and would also be performing, in addition to the Mass, four Psalms and four Commandments.

The story went on to recall the confusion of 'that fateful day' when the Mass was first performed by these now-popular bands and likened the Borrominian Oratorio San Filippo to a bus at rush hour.

It reminded its readers of the debate that resulted immediately the Mass finished and how both the press and the clergy were divided, one side against and one in favour.

*Ciao Amici* also reminded its readers they had predicted the discourse would restart as it had not been resolved since the Mass, neither within the walls of the Borrominian Hall or in the newspapers lead stories of the following days.

Was this a prophecy of what was to happen with the tour?

The details of the tour were included in the article:

> *The debut will be on September 11 in the United Kingdom: the home of the music beats. In London, the Mass will be performed in the Royal Albert Hall.*
>
> *After England, the groups will make a three week tour that will take them to Belgium, Holland and Scandinavia.*
> *The sacred temple of music beats, the Olympia of Paris, should host the spiritual concert. Negotiations in this direction are already underway and almost certainly will result in a positive outcome.*
>
> *That is not all. Other requests were coming in from overseas and so next spring the three groups will be on Broadway.*

The program for the tour was in two parts, with the first part being the added Psalms and four Commandments and the second part the actual Mass as presented in Rome.

The Psalms were: *Happy is the man, There is no God, The Lord is my shepherd* and *Sing to the Lord,* while the four Commandments were: *The only God (I am the Lord your God) Thou shalt not kill, God is truth (Do not bear false witness)* and *The Woman of Others (Do not desire the woman of others).*

The newspaper stated that other countries also wanted to participate in a discussion involving not only Italian music and young people, but music generally and youth around the world, and that the Catholic youth of the world especially wanted to join in the debate about the renewal and progress within the church.

The band had quickly settled into their amazing new rehearsal venue and were combining touring Italy and practising for the tour.

# 9. Vatican interference and obstruction

The Vatican had made no attempt to prevent the Mass from going ahead and there appears no record of it even questioning the concept. However, the Church were now faced with priests arguing among themselves and newspaper reports stridently criticising the Mass, particularly in Italy and France

One low point in the media war saw everyone involved —organisers, composer and bands— labelled Fascists simply because the only newspaper to come out in support of the Mass was an extreme right wing one.

## *Excommunication*

In the face of all this controversy, the Vatican decided the fallout from the Mass was too damaging for the Church, and resolved to act to show it did not support this new form of music in the church. The action that was taken was inconsiderate, hurtful and cold hearted, and Angel and the Brains discovered quickly how unthinking and harsh Vatican decisions can be.

The young priest Anselmo, who had helped Father Sinaldi with the organisation, arrived at the theatre a few weeks after the Mass and told the boys that they had been excommunicated because of their participation in the Mass.

The boys were astounded. How could someone be excommunicated for following respected, leading Church officials and participating in an event that was the Church's idea? They had performed music that the Church had given them to perform, they hadn't blasphemed, they hadn't sinned.

According to the Catholic Encyclopaedia, excommunication is the most serious penalty that the Church can inflict onto members of the church who have committed a very grave offence. Excommunication is considered a medicinal rather than a vindictive penalty, intended, not so much to punish the culprit, as to correct him and bring him back to the path of righteousness.

Understanding the relevance of excommunication, Angelo's father, who was there as the band's manager at the time, was aghast and just kept repeating, "But why?"

It should be remembered that three of the Church officials involved in the Mass were Father Sinaldi, a Dominican priest whose order specialised working with young people and two of the lyric writers, Father Charles Gasbarri and Professor Tommaso

Federici. At the time Gasbarri was editor of the Vatican newspaper *L'Osservatore Romano* and Professor Tommaso Federici was with the Pontifical Liturgical Institute

When Father Anselmo left, the boys discussed their situation. Although they were all Catholics, none of them was particularly religious. So, excommunication meant they couldn't attend church services? They shrugged; big deal, they weren't really keen on going to church services anyway, with its traditional songs and music and rhythms. They were rock and roll musicians and they had better things to do than worry about attending a Church for which they had done their best and been betrayed. If excommunication were the worst that the Church could visit upon them—whether they had deserved it or not—they were unmoved and largely indifferent.

Unfortunately for the boys, excommunication was only the first weapon in the Church's arsenal, and what followed over the next few months would affect them very much.

An Italian paper ran the story of the boys' excommunication but Angelo believes that the story has disappeared from the archives.

It was just the beginning.

Their excommunication lasted less than a month. Pressure brought to bear on the Church from international newspaper articles demanding an explanation from the Vatican about the excommunication brought about a rescinding of the order, although Angel and the Brains were told that the Pope had reconsidered.

The second in charge of Santa Croce in Gerusalemme Church visited them just a few weeks later to advise that they had been reinstated and forgiven, but the Vatican had decreed that henceforth they were not allowed to play electric guitars or drums in a Catholic church again.

Again, according to the Catholic Encyclopaedia, a person excommunicated is considered an exile from Christian society but the exile can be removed as soon as the offender has given 'suitable satisfaction'.

While they understood its severity in the eyes of the church and the Catholic community, the band had taken no action on their excommunication, nor had they changed their ways or asked for forgiveness, so they could not be considered to have given 'suitable satisfaction'.

Was the lifting of the excommunication an admittance of the Vatican's wrong decision or did it position the church for more serious retribution?

The boys took it all in their stride, believing all was right with the world. Summer was going well with bookings at plenty of concerts, and the promised tour was still ahead. The Mass would be performed in concert halls not churches abroad, so there should be no problem with the latest decree that electric guitars and drums could not be played in a Church. The band thought that everything had been sorted out favourably and that nothing would change.

How wrong could they have been?

### *World tour cancelled*

The next episode in this curious string of 'consequences' was when they heard the tour had been cancelled.

At the end of August, Angelo received a phone call from by Piero Ciampi, artistic director of Ariel recording company.

"Hi Angelo, I'm sorry to tell you this but the tour has been cancelled. Giombini didn't have the courage to call you himself. He is very disappointed."

"Why, what happened?" asked Angelo.

"I really don't know, looks like all the promoters have backed out of the project for some reason but I don't know exactly why," replied Ciampi.

The downward slide had started.

The tour had been due to commence in early September, a scant few weeks away.

Was the decision to cancel the tour made by the individual governments overseas or did it come directly from the Vatican?

It is highly unlikely that, by coincidence, all countries would make the same decision at the same time—especially Japan—without influence having been brought to bear from somewhere.

At that time the Catholic Church had been in conferences with the Anglican Church, the Protestants and the Orthodox Church as part of the outcomes of Vatican II. They had agreed to a common friendship and peaceful line of view.

What Angelo and I have been able to confirm through different sources is that the tour was cancelled because the Vatican used its enormous influence by asking—or quite likely in some cases, instructing—the government of each country not to permit the Mass concert to be performed. With nowhere to perform, and an unpopular project, the promoters quickly retreated.

Although the influence of the Vatican in France, with more Catholics than even in Italy, and in the Christian countries of England and the United States is easily understandable, the cancellation of the Japanese leg of the tour is less readily explicable. We can only assume it was because there was a strong American influence in Japan, including large contingents of soldiers coming and going to Vietnam, and that the pressure on Japan came via the USA.

This not only affected the three bands directly involved with the Mass, but also all the support teams—the road crews, lighting and sound technicians and many others who would been needed to accompany the tour.

To this day some sources claim, quite erroneously, that it was the record company's fault for the cancellation of the tour. Ariel had nothing to do with the tour; they were only involved in producing the record.

### Nowhere to practice

It was about October 1966 when the boys were told they could no longer use the cathedral for their practice sessions.

"But where will we practice?" the boys asked the monsignor, hurt and bewildered.

"What have we done wrong?" They could only see that they had done as the Church had asked them. They had performed the Church's songs in their own style, they had enticed young people to the concert, was this not what Vatican II was all about?

But the monsignor could only shake his head sadly at them and shrug. "You need to find another place to practise," was all he could say to them, "or I shall be in trouble too."

A friend helped them find an alternative rehearsal room in the basement of an apartment block, owned by a freelance photographer. An artisans' block, where people made things to sell, the basement had its own entrance and although the boys felt that they were back where they started, in a dark and gloomy basement instead of their light-filled cathedral with its stage and great acoustics, they acknowledged that it was still larger than their original basement rehearsal room.

"Here we go again" thought Angelo. "This is very depressing."

He recalled that the front door lock was not secure enough and because the locksmith couldn't come straight away to change it they slept there for a couple nights, wary of thieves and fearing for the safety of their instruments.

### Priests

The priests involved in the Mass were not immune to the actions of the Vatican either. The young priest Anselmo, who had assisted Father Sinaldi, was sent to a remote town in South America. Father Sinaldi, who had soon expected to rise to the post of cardinal, ended up in Tuscany.

It is timely to remember the words of Father Sinaldi when he opened the concert, "In a hard and merciless era like ours, a profane music can be useful in expressing religious sentiments—although I want to assure you that the promoters of this enterprise have absolutely no intention of putting light music into the church's official cult, that is, its worship."

Many felt that the 'hard and merciless' world Father Sinaldi referred to was being caused by the Vatican.

### Concerts stop

Then, as quickly as fame arrived, it disappeared. The band's Naples manager, who had organised many of their concerts, could not fathom why in October he was suddenly unable get any bookings for them at all.

The boys asked, "Why is this happening all of a sudden?"

"I don't know. There is no one prepared to put you inside a hall again," replied the mystified manager.

At this time of year, as the autumn was beginning to turn cold, concerts were no longer being held in outdoor venues, but were booked instead for the warmer concert halls.

The manager added, "There is only one gig I can offer you but that is in Tunisia."

When I questioned Angelo about whether the band had changed its style or if it had simply been the end of their style of music, Angelo was quick to say, "It doesn't happen that quickly. Not when you are doing concerts with 30,000 people in the square jumping up and down like mad and you're doing that in town after town after town after town."

Excommunication, a world tour cancelled, music careers almost shattered and severe disappointment and even anger with the Catholic Church did not stop Giombini and the bands hoping that the extensive tour could be revived.

In September, despite the obstacles in their way, Angel and the Brains recorded the soundtrack *When You Went Away* for the movie *Blueprint for a Massacre*. They were happy to get this job and hoped that their run of bad luck was over, that they would be able to shake the stigma of being involved with the Mass.

It didn't help. The band's name was synonymous with that fateful Mass.

The boys tried to ascertain from newspapers and the television station if anyone knew why they were suddenly anathema, treated like nobodies, as though no-one had ever heard of Angel and the Brains. It was like their band had been wiped from the memory of every brain in Italy.

They were disheartened and disillusioned. All they had ever wanted was to play music—not play politics.

### *Ariel closes*

Ariel was the next casualty. It was a very small record company and had put an enormous amount of money into the production, marketing and advertising of the records from the Mass, only to suddenly find they couldn't sell the records anywhere. With the little bit of money left they tried to change direction, but their realisation of their peril was too late. They closed due to financial hardship.

# 10. New successes, new challenges and new set backs

## Tunisia

Because they were unable to get a new contract, the band decided to go to Africa and spent Christmas and New Year there.

Unfortunately, this decision was the start of the band braking up. Maurizio Vitti chose not to go with them; he refused to believe that the group couldn't get further contracts in Italy and of all the members of the band he was the most depressed and disillusioned by the aftermath of the Mass.

This meant that the band needed to find another guitar player. There was not enough time to hold an audition, but Maurizio Aloisi knew of someone who could play, so they asked him to join. They discovered that he wasn't the best guitar player, but by this time they were desperate.

By this time The Brains' performance at these concerts included movie tracks and they had started to play some of the songs of Led Zeppelin and other similar, popular groups.

One of their concerts was held at the Hilton Hotel in Tunis, which was very expensive.

The manager of the hotel, perhaps not understanding the music or the background of the group, expected that all the patrons would be over thirty years old.

However, there was a strong French influence in Tunisia at the time, and the boys' fame and the popularity of their music had spread following the Mass. The hotel was overwhelmed by the response of the younger generation, which saw a considerable number of young people present at the concert, while many more were turned away at the door because of a shortage of seating.

The more mature members of the audience just sat and enjoyed the music, decorously clapping their hands now and then, but many of the younger audience members stood up to dance.

This was not becoming to a hotel of the Hilton's standard where the manager would not tolerate guests making a 'spectacle' of themselves. These 'unruly' patrons were told to behave or they would need to leave.

On their return from North Africa in January 1967, there were still no contracts available for them in Italy and this situation went on from month to month to month. Nobody was prepared to let them play inside a venue.

Before the start of summer, they again had an offer to play in Tunisia, this time for three months. For the first time, uncertainty and stress caused arguments to start between the band members. The debate within the band raged: should they wait to see if this summer would improve their chances in Italy, or should they cut their losses and return to Africa?

Ruggero stood firm, refusing to go back to Africa. But Angelo and the others felt that they might have more chance elsewhere and so reluctantly he and the others decided to remain four elements in the band and returned to Africa.

By the time the contract in Africa was finished, however, the four remaining band members were at loggerheads again. Angelo was tired of Africa and was determined to return to Italy and pursue their careers there, while the others were tempted by another six-month contract in Africa. In the end, Angelo returned home and the three remaining Brains members stayed. The band had broken up.

Those band members that had remained stayed in Tunisia for a couple of months and then they too returned in Italy. Maurizio Aloisi joined the Pecore Nere group and Alberto Del Duca joined the Maya group.

### *B2000*

Another band, Boeing 2000, was having similar problems within their group and a few of them approached Angelo about forming a new band together.

Believing that the fiasco following the Mass would not impact on the new band because only two members of Angel and the Brains were now playing together and the band's name would change completely, Angelo was positive about the idea. Once he learned that these players were into Rhythm and Blues, playing the songs of Wilson Pickett, Otis

Reading and Joe Tex (among others), he was ecstatic. These were his music heroes at that time.

The remaining two members of Angel and the Brains, Angelo and Maurizio, along with three from Boeing 2000 combined. They picked up two saxophone players and a keyboard player to form the band B2000 playing Rhythm and Blues. The new band became very popular and all indications were that it would be very successful.

The B2000 featured a lead singer who was small in stature but had a big voice and Angelo stayed on the drums. They began to get some good gigs again and toward the end of a contract at the Titan Club, the biggest disco club in Rome, their manager announced he had a contract for them in Japan playing R&B for three months.

### New arguments

Angelo recalls, "We wanted to grab it. Going around Japan for three months playing Rhythm & Blues and earning big money sounded like a dream, but Franchino, the singer, decided that he didn't want to go because our record company had also told us they would be ready for us to make our first record in a month's time."

Once again the arguments started.

Angelo and another band member tried to keep the peace by saying there was plenty of time to do both the tour and the record. Having the tour and the record meant they wouldn't need to look for work for at least another year. They didn't want to break up but the fights continued. Eventually the keyboard player walked out after abusing the rest of the band members.

Another member said he had spoken to the manager who told him, "We can wait three months. It is good money, do the tour then cut your record when you come back."

The little singer exploded! "How dare you go behind our backs and talk to him without the rest of us."

While the rest of the band agreed that it did not matter whether one of them or all of them had got the promise from the manager that the record could be done when they returned from Japan, the singer would not be placated, and refused to go on tour, demanding that the record come first.

Unfortunately, without their lead singer, who was incredibly popular with all the young people, the band could no longer continue.

The band folded. "We didn't go on tour, we didn't do the record," Angelo told me sadly. "Because of the arguments we lost the two saxophone players and then the guitar player. I did understand them.

At that point we all needed money even more than success and the tour in Japan was more important than the record."

It was 1968, Angelo considered his short music career was over and became a sales representative with a music instrument company.

## 11. The church and the media since 1966

The debate that started on 27th April 1966 continues to this day and often the media reports are vicious and bitter. The focus is always on whether the Mass should ever had been held or if modern music has a place in the Church and I wonder how many people question what actually happened following the event.

Did any of the young people that acclaimed their music in 1966 ever ask why Angel and the Brains and the Bumpers didn't continue to perform or make records?

Did the Vatican and the media ever give a single thought to the damage they were doing to innocent participants in their experiment; damage that was sustained through their continued arguments, cover ups and secrecy?

Has anyone ever stopped to wonder why they are unable to find reports about the success or otherwise of the 'world tour' of the Mass? Because there was no announcement or report that the tour had been cancelled, several articles claim that the bands completed the tour. Even the respected Italian music historian, Tiziano Tarli, seems to imply in his book *Italian Beat* that the tour went ahead.

Even more recently it seems people are still reluctant to speak about what happened following the Mass. In an interview, a member of one of the other bands would not explain what had happened with the tour.

Angel and the Brains had been good Catholic boys who had been led to believe that they were playing an important role in bringing the church to young people; that is until the actions of the Vatican not only destroyed their faith in the church but their careers.

It would be easy to fill another book just with summaries of the discussions, debates and arguments over the last forty-seven years in both religious and music circles but I have included just a few examples.

In 2007 the Italian newspaper *La Repubblica* reported:

> *During the 1960s in Rome, we witnessed the phenomenon of the so-called 'Beat Mass'. It had the effect of a nuclear meltdown, with the fatal consequence of recognising the 'right to liturgical citizenship' of a practice as dangerous as it was reckless. That is to say, liturgical music now could be - or even must be? - a simple transposition of the profane music then in style.*

*Mass-market music—inconsistent, insipid, and ephemeral— was then erroneously and unjustly dubbed 'popular', just as its disconcerting, clamorous, noisy, twisted manifestations that so delighted huge, undiscerning crowds were erroneously called 'concerts'. It is precisely this false 'popular' genre, imposed by the overwhelming force of the means of communication at the service of unscrupulous vendors that has dried up the pure springs of Gregorian chant and of cultured popular music that constitute the most beautiful decoration of our churches and celebrations.*

*La Repubblica* carried another article titled Rock Mass returns in the church with electric guitar on 24th May 2008. The following are extracts from the article:

*............ what had become of the 'mass beats', with electric guitars and keyboards in the church, with the boys ready to sing, perhaps with their hair a bit longer than was lawful at that time?*

The article continues with a description of similar rock Masses being held around the world and then continues to recall the event of 1966.

*It was the same 45 years ago, in 1963, when the phenomenon of 'beat' also took hold in Italy. The boys began growing their hair, playing electric guitars, living and dressing differently to their parents.*

*The phenomenon spread like wild oil, to frequently find next to the altar in the churches the instruments of a youth band..............*

This is true but it didn't begin to happen until many years after the 1966 event.

*"A small altar facing the people and a group of young men who, placed on one side of the aisle, gave vent to a certain number of decibels emitted by their amplified instruments: this was the first meeting with the liturgical reform desired by Vatican II remained in my memory as a child in the mid-60s," says Massimo Nosetti today organist of the Cathedral of Turin. "The astonished faithful were reassured by the good priest that this was the new way desired by the Church, I remember his exact words, 'to help the faithful to participate more fully.'"*

If it was the original Beat Mass in 1966 that Mr Nosetti recalls, his memory of the staging is incorrect. If the reader refers to the earlier photo taken inside the Oratorium it can be seen that there was a large stage with all three bands.

The article continues

*It was an extraordinary season, until the early
seventies. Then slowly guitars and keyboards
disappeared from the liturgy, but the rock has,
in some ways, remained, as demonstrated by
John Paul II, when on September 27th 1997 he
was with Bob Dylan in Bologna to celebrate
the Eucharistic Congress. Pope Ratzinger [Pope
Benedict XVI] was sceptical about that choice
and has said so publicly.*

The newspaper is wrong here. The 'season' certainly
didn't continue until the early seventies. It ended
within six months of the Mass. In fact the newspaper
itself played a role in that with its negative reporting.

*On rock music in church Benedict XVI had
doubts: "Really, in the liturgy we cannot say
that one song is equal to another. In this regard,
it should avoid generic improvisation or the
introduction of musical genres which fail to
respect the meaning of the liturgy."*

On 4th–6th May 2012 an International Liturgical
Congress titled 'The Pontifical Institute—between
Memory and Prophecy' was held in Rome to observe
the 50th anniversary of the 1961 founding of the
Pontifical Liturgical Institute. In his address to the
group, Pope Benedict XVI stated that the liturgy lives

from a healthy tradition integrated with legitimate progress.

"With these two terms," he said, "the Council Fathers wished to deliver their program of reform, in harmony with the liturgical tradition of the past and the future," though he also noted that the experience of the past decades shows that tradition and progress have often been 'awkwardly contrasted'.

There could be no greater understatement than 'awkwardly contrasted' when the treatment handed out to Marcello Giombini and the bands who performed *La Messa dei Giovani* is studied.

Following the success of the Mass, a world tour was planned. Firstly Paris, then London, Belgium, Holland, Scandinavia and then New York and Tokyo and back in Milan. There was also some discussion to have one in Frankfurt, Madrid and in Montreal. Instead, the tour was cancelled, a record company went bankrupt, leading luminaries of the reform were punished with distant or poor postings, and the careers of the musicians fatally damaged.

'Progress' as a result of Vatican II has continually been talked about by the church for 50 years and nothing really has been done with the exception of the Mass not having to be in Latin but is allowed to be in the language of the country and improved communication with other religions.

In relation to 'admitting all forms of art' there has been progress but it has taken 50 years, which is little consolation to those involved in 1966. Today we see guitars, keyboards and drums in churches. It took decades after the original Mass before some churches let those instruments in again. We note that Beat Masses are popular today and many are held in many Catholic churches but we have not been able to find reference to any being held in Rome.

## 12. But the music lives on

### *Art form*

Vatican II was supposed to have changed things, especially in attracting young people back to the church. It approved and admitted all forms of art that had an appropriate quality. Holy music in any form is to the glory of god and the certification of the believers but the Pope put his finger on it.

As mentioned before, none of the criticism immediately after the Mass actually judged the success of the 'experiment' in line with its aim of attracting young people to the church.

Who is to judge what 'art' is and what is 'appropriate quality'? We found several definitions of music as an art form and many refer to music as the science or art of ordering tones or sounds in succession, in combination, and in temporal relationships to produce a composition having unity and continuity.

Certainly there were people at the time who considered the work of maestro Giombini and the bands he chose to perform his music as being musical pioneers. It is also fortunate that today there are young people who have an appreciation of the quality of the music, recognise the significant contribution to Italian modern music they made and keep it alive through current technology.

There are websites, blogs and Facebook pages paying to tribute to the original bands and those that followed in their musical footsteps.

Young people, especially in Italy, still consider the album from the Mass to be a significant work in the history of music. In 2012 a young Italian wrote in his blog:

> *Great record! Even if (and it is not the first time I have said it) I do not like the Catholic Church argument! but looking further, I say that these three bands in the performance and their technique is amazing!*

We have not found any debate about the artistic qualities of the music. Surely the test of time has confirmed that Giombini's compositions and the way they were interpreted by the bands in 1966 attest to it being a work of art.

### The name of Angel and the Brains lives on

Although Angel and the Brains disbanded early, their name still lives on in 2013. Their records are highly collectable and still reach good prices through online auctions. Video clips of the band and the music from the Mass have been uploaded onto YouTube as recently as 2012. These posts often ask for more information or recall fond memories.

Because the Ariel record label folded, the band has never received any royalties from any of the records they produced under that label.

Obviously, when the records were first released, they attracted a lot of interest because of the enthralling beat sound of the compositions by Giombini and the bands' interpretation of his music.

At the time of the Italian release of the LP, *Time Magazine* gave it this review:

> *The Mass of the Young is about as far out as an LP can get. Three big-beat groups sing an entire Mass accompanied by electric guitars. The Latins call it the Messa Ye Ye, and it had its world premiere April 27 in a Rome church while youngsters frugged in the aisles and priests clapped hands. (July 6, 1966)*

One post we found on a YouTube clip says:

> *I don't have "La Messa Dei Giovani" but I can say that at least one of the tracks ("Graduale" by The Brains) is a great punker, paradoxically with religious lyrics. The whole LP was supposed to*

> have a religious character, and it does, as you can
> tell from the titles of the songs -- it's something
> like a Christian rock extravaganza... I have
> "Graduale" on a single but it's also on the "Only
> For Real Losers" compilation that came out a
> couple of years ago.

In fact it was so successful it is reported that the album was reprinted several times:

> ...two years later by Bluebell (with different
> cover); also in 1968 by the Associated Producers
> as "folk-Mass the Mass of young people" (and
> another different cover) and in 1969 from the
> Roman Record Company (with a cover the same
> as the Ariel one).

Angel and the Brains have also never received any royalties from these re-released albums.

Original copies of the albums are highly collectable and sought after by more than just the teen generation of the 60s. The performance that started as religious music has developed a cult following that can be experienced at hard core beat concerts around the world.

Songs by Angel and the Brains have also been included on compilation albums often referred to as Garage Beat music.

In 1999 *Only for Real Losers* was released under the More label featuring Angel and the Brains singing *"Graduale"* from the Mass.

The album *Per Chi Non Conosce la Liberta (For those who do not know the Liberty)* on the Reverend Moon label in 1995, not only includes *San Francesco* (one of the additional songs planned for the world tour) by Angel and the Brains, but their photo features on the cover.

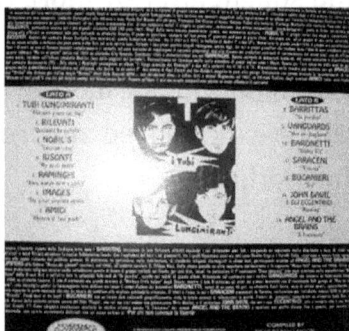

Again, the bands have never received any royalties from these compilation albums.

Beat Masses have been held in recent years in Italy including 2008 at the Shrine of Our Lady of the Gate of Guastalla (Reggio Emilia), 2009 at Church of St. Maria Assunta in Cafaggio (Prato) and 2012 at Church of San Vitale Martyr in Salsomaggiore Terme (Parma). There are many other examples of rock Masses being held elsewhere in the world.

However, most references to today's beat sound acknowledge Giombini's work as the best and most inspired and the bands that performed his Mass in 1966 as the finest examples of Italian beat.

It is a ludicrous and ironic situation when stories of these Masses cite the 1966 event as the first and most successful and give credit to the Vatican II council for encouraging them as a way of bringing young people to the Church.

Forty-seven years later, guitars are being played in churches when in 1966 it was decreed that guitars and drums were not allowed inside the Church for any reason.

*The Messa Dei Giovani* was a well-intentioned experiment by respected individuals of the Catholic Church to bring young people back into the fold.

The actions of the Vatican not only prevented that from happening but impacted on a group of young people (from the very section of the population they were trying to reach) and caused their music careers to suffer following the Mass.

Bands still record and perform songs either from the Mass or in the 'beat' style. In 2011 a Roman band, and one of the best exponents of Italian Beat today, the Illuminati, released an LP titled 'Take the Guitar and Pray'. The title is a direct reference to the slogan Giombini had coined for the Mass and includes brilliant versions of *Graduale* and *Gloria* from *La Messa dei Giovani*.

### Beat Mass in Salsomaggiore Terme

It was announced that On Sunday, 1st July 2012 'The sound of the Beat Mass will be repeated in the religious function performed by the Band Tony Borlotti & his flauers (Salerno).
The venue was the Crypt of the Church of San Vitale Martyr Salsomaggiore Terme (Pr)'.

The announcement also stated:

> *Presentation meeting: The phenomenon of the Italian Beat Masses. From the Second Vatican Council to hippies in the sacristy.*

*Following will be the preview of the documentary 'Let my cry come to you' (Beat Records) to be released in October 2012. History of Italian Beat Masses. Guests Dario Salvatori (music critic and journalist RAI) and Tiziano Tarli (music historian and guitarist of the Illuminati). Moderator Gino Delledonne*

*It was April 27th 1966 when the Mass of the Young was performed for the first time at the Borrominian Oratory of St. Philip Neri at the Vallicella (Rome). Between 1962 and 1965 was held the Second Vatican Council, which was a real 'new springtime' of Christianity. Its own innovations, and in particular the subsequent liturgical reform, stimulated composers to compose songs with sounds beats. And young priests opened the doors of their Oratoriums to groups, to bring close, also with music, the youth to the Church.*

*Among the most well-known composers, inspired and fruitful in this new form of sacred music, there was the maestro Marcello Giombini (1928 - 2003), the most known bands that dedicated themselves to this music were the Barrittas, Angel & the Brains and the Bumpers; The finest records "The Mass of the young ", "Cantata of the third world" and 'Psalms for Our Time'.*

*Today the Mass played in pure beat style, comes back as the protagonist of the Beat Festival which will be held from June 27 to July 1, 2012, in Salsomaggiore Terme (Parma).*

This announcement acknowledges the greatness of Giombini's music and the quality of the bands on 27th April 1966, but that time can hardly be called a 'new springtime'. The period after the Mass was more like a sparkling autumn that led into a cold and miserable winter.

# 13. Angelo blames the church

### *Angelo moves to Australia*

The end of Angelo's music career was reinforced with his marriage in April 1969, as his wife did not support his music career. The end of his music is something he still mourns today. He and his wife moved to Australia in 1970.

In 1974 two more members from Angels and the Brains also migrated to Australia and got together with another musician playing in an outer suburb of Sydney restaurant.

They asked Angelo to join them but again he found their style boring and didn't continue when the contract finished. In the 1970s Italian bands in Australia played regional folkloric Italian songs mostly from the Neapolitan or southern areas of Italy, or they played very old Italian ballads. This was more or less to be expected as most of the Italian migrants in Australia had been post-war migrants from those areas of Italy.

He took up the drums for a young keyboard player for another two months in 1974 because at the time he needed the money, but his wife hated him being out at nights playing, so he eventually concentrated on his day job and forgot about his music.

As an Italian migrant with limited English, he found it difficult to get into the style of band he would have liked and the only option available to him was to play the music he had resisted so strongly as a young teenager.

He remarried in 1988, and although his second wife was a lot more encouraging and wanted Angelo to take up his music again, by this time he felt the stigma of migrants was too strong. While he was confident that his drumming skills were equal or better than those in the bands around, he felt like an outsider, as though he was not welcome because he was not like them.

He agrees that today it is a different story in Australia and a good drummer regardless of his origins would be welcome into the Australian music scene.

This has been a difficult story for Angelo to tell. It has only been through the encouragement of his present wife and his son that it has been made possible.

Angelo told me, "Still today I would like one of the promoters to come forward and tell me why.

"It seemed that every country feared the repercussions of going against the Vatican, just as an individual person would fear the repercussions of going against the Mafia.

Was the Vatican simply the world's dictator?"

Angel and the Brains could not get any more contracts in Italy ....Why? The Vatican had so much power and influence in Italy it was able to scare off organisers, promoters, venue owners and managers and not to give them gigs.

They were doomed not just in Italy but in most Christian countries and many others.

Angelo told me, "We were doomed by the Mass because the Vatican was ready to do anything to destroy us as musicians. The same happened to the Bumpers. The Barrittas had retreated to Sardinia and their name was never mentioned for a while. They would have been playing small venues in Sardinia."

In researching this book, apart from the Mass, the only reference we could find concerning the Bumpers music is a single record, Cupitadion, on Youtube. It is sad that the description is simply 'Roman Superband of the 60s, advocates of an amazing garage beat. Great and unknown Roman 60s garage band".

The band members had underestimated the power of the Vatican when it has its mind set on looking after its own image and reputation before anything else.

Angelo recalled, "There was a lot of disaster coming from the Vatican and the so-called sticky idiots of Catholic people against us. When they caused the concerts around Europe and in Japan to be cancelled was when we really started to question the church that we had grown up part of."

"Initially the Mass was good publicity for the band but by 1967 we figured out that unfortunately the Mass was our destruction because of the bad publicity and because no-one wanted to know about us."

"Once we realised that we took 'Angel' out of our name so the band became simply 'The Brains'. But even that didn't help.

"Every manager around and everyone in the music industry had in their mind 'they are the Mass people you don't touch them'. That's how we ended up in Africa. Unfortunately ending up in Africa meant the end of the group."

I questioned Angelo about whether this really happened.

"We had been invited by a Catholic priest to perform a Catholic Mass in a Catholic church. We were young and naïve. We believed that what a small group of senior priests were organising would have been with the blessing of the whole Catholic Church. Why did we, young and talented musicians, have to have our careers destroyed because the Church couldn't agree within its own people and hierarchy?"

He pointed out, "The truth is simple, and you only need to look at the series of events.

- Angel and the Brains could not get any more contracts in Italy

- Ariel had to close

- Some priests involved directly in the Mass were sent elsewhere

- Every country coincidentally pulled out of the world tour

- Angel and the Brains had to leave the theatre where they were practicing because it was owned by the Catholic Church

- Giombini retired in Assisi for several years

- A Mass Beat has never again been played in any place (not just Churches) in Rome."

This was the first Beat Mass in religious music history and created for male voices, electric guitars, bass, organ and percussions. *La Messa dei Giovanni* was the first of the six Masses composed by Marcello Giombini but considered his most splendid. However, it would be some time before Giombini returned to writing religious music and the additional new Masses. It was from this first creation of Giombini's that the Italian beat really grew momentum.

Many authors and journalists writing about this period of Italian music and the Italian Beat credit the Barrittas with creating the beat. The Barrittas had nothing to do with the beat even for the Mass. The only true beat bands then were Angel and the Brains and the Bumpers.

## 14. Author's final note

It may appear that the story told in this book is a criticism of the Catholic Church generally. This is not the case. The accusations in this story specifically relate to the actions of the Vatican and the Church hierarchy immediately following the Mass and the impact they had on the innocent participants.

We found many articles about the Mass spanning over 50 years. It seems that the truth and the facts have been lost in time—or perhaps they were purposely buried.

In several stories it gives the impression that the Barrittas were totally responsible for the Mass and I hope that at least the more recent authors will now correct their stories.

Maestro Giombini composed the music and it was performed and recorded on the original album, by three bands, The Barrittas, the Bumpers and Angel and the Brains.

As mentioned earlier in the book, the maestro encouraged the bands to perform his music in their own style. This resulted in Angel and the Brains and the Bumpers creating the Italian Beat sound partly inspired by the compositions of the maestro.

If you re-read the descriptions of the songs you will see that this was the case. Better still, get a copy of the original recording and judge for yourself.

It is time Angel and the Brains and the Bumpers received due recognition for their contribution to not only Italian music but world music.

I hope this book helps to put history straight in that regard but, more importantly, clears up any misdirected belief that the young bands knowingly did anything in contravention of Church policy or beliefs.

I want readers to realise that those young men were the victims of Catholic Church action that has haunted them for 50 years.

I leave the last word to the great man who did everything in his power to make the Catholic Church relevant to the modern world. On his deathbed Pope John XXIII reportedly stated:

> *Today more than ever ... we are called to serve man as such, and not merely Catholics; to defend above all and everywhere the rights of the human person, and not merely those of the Catholic Church.*

*Today's world, the needs made plain in the last fifty years and a deeper understanding of doctrine have brought us to a new situation ... It is not that the Gospel has changed, it is that we have begun to understand it better.*

*Those who have lived as long as I have ...were enabled to compare different cultures and traditions, and know that the moment has come to discern the signs of the times, to seize the opportunity and to look far ahead.*

www.ingramcontent.com/pod-product-compliance
Lightning Source LLC
Chambersburg PA
CBHW060257050426
42448CB00009B/1671